Tao Te Ching
Lao Tzu

An Intuitive Interpretation by Robert M. Jankel

Bambaz Press
Los Angeles CA

Acknowledgements:
I thank my wife, Carolinda, who has supported me continuously over the years.

Also, I want to acknowledge my close friends Michael Topp and Rena Shpegel who have given me suggestions on this book.

In addition, I'd like to thank Bambi and Baz from BAMBAZ Press for making this book a reality.

Copyright ©2018 by Robert M. Jankel
All Rights Reserved
Printed in the United States of America

Cover Design: Baz Here
Book Design and Artwork: Robert M. Jankel
Edited by Bambi Here

ISBN: 9781724451484

Bambaz Press
548 S Spring Street
Suite 1201
Los Angeles, CA
90013
contact: Bambi@bambazpress.com

Tao Te Ching—i

About the Author Lao Tzu

The Tao Te Ching is a very old book of wisdom, but little is known about the author, Lao Tzu. Some people believe that he was born as much as one hundred years before Confucius. Others postulate that Lao Tzu was a contemporary of Confucius and that the two men had met one another. As the legend has it, Lao Tzu held the position of archivist at the Imperial Court in Lo Yang, in the province of Honan, China. As he grew older, Lao Tzu became disenchanted with his life and with the chaotic ways of the people around him, and he decided to leave the Imperial Court to embrace a secluded life in the country.

However, as the legend goes, this remains conjecture. As for any historical proof, Lao Tzu remains a mystery. As a matter of fact, the use of the word "author" may be misleading. It's quite possible that the Tao Te Ching was orally transmitted which would explain why there are variations in different versions. Perhaps fifty to a hundred years passed before it was written down. The proof may be found in Poem Eighty where it says, "Let the people tie knots in rope instead of writing…"

As to when the Tao Te Ching came into existence, I believe that Lao Tzu or its creators were contemporaries of Confucius. That means it could have come into existence a bit before 500 BC or somewhat after. Of course, I could be mistaken about dates, but it does seem that a number of the poems are reactions to Confucian beliefs. So, it's my opinion that the Tao Te Ching was created when Confucius was still living or perhaps a bit after his death. Confucius was born in 551 BC and died in 479 BC, but keep in mind, if it was originally transmitted orally, it may not have been written down for fifty to one hundred years later.

Why I've Reinterpreted the Book

For more than two decades I had been contemplating translations of an ancient Chinese book, the Tao Te Ching. The Tao Te Ching addresses, in symbolic terms, how one can achieve spiritual wholeness. However, the translations tend to be either scholarly or poetic. The former approach sounds literal and stiff; the latter approach sometimes lacks substance. As I reflected on these differences, I came to recognize that two versions would promote greater insight into the meaning of the Tao Te Ching. This would include a "somewhat orthodox" version along with one that would redefine, simplify or "read between the lines." From comparing both texts, a reader would be able to gain better understanding of its wisdom. I began to write my own interpretation of the Tao Te Ching using this two-pronged approach. To do this, I used English translations. Sometimes each book would say essentially the same things for a specific passage, and sometimes each book would say something contradictory for another section.

To achieve clarity, I relied heavily on the ancient Chinese book, the I-Ching. In fact, I've often said that the I-Ching acted as my translator. Interestingly, some scholars believe that Lao Tzu used the I-Ching extensively when he was working on the Tao Te Ching. Regardless, I am indebted to the I-Ching for giving me direction.

How I Became Interested in the Tao Te Ching

At the age of seventeen I went through a difficult time of looking for answers. I wanted to know if there really was a "God" or a "Supreme Being." Was there a purpose to my life? Finally, after months of thinking, reading, questioning, and sincerely searching, one day, I told myself that I hadn't discovered anything. I was so frustrated that I began to cry. Later, somewhere between sleeping and waking, something happened to me. I don't know exactly how to explain it. For a moment, I lost myself. For a moment (or was it longer?) so much passed through me that I couldn't possibly hold on to it. All I can tell you is that for me there was such an answer! This answer, however, wasn't communicated with words. It was nothing like that. For a time, after this experience, I tried to make some sense of what had happened to me. I searched for explanations.

A few years after this occurrence, I bought two translations of the Tao Te Ching. Here was a book that spoke about things that I had experienced and had been thinking about. Yet, after reading certain poems and not being satisfied that I had grasped the essence of what was being said, I compared the poetic version with the more literal translation and came away with a better understanding.

Tao Te Ching—iv

Using Two Versions to Solve the Enigma of Poem Five

Using two versions of one poem, let's examine the fifth poem in my version of the Tao Te Ching:

Five

Heaven and earth are not humane
and perceive the ten thousand beings as straw dogs.
The wise person is not humane
and perceives the people as straw dogs.

It's that space between heaven and earth,
isn't it like a bellows,
empty—yet not devoid of life.
Move it back and forth and never stop using it.
Talk too much and you become exhausted.
Better hold tightly to what you already have within.

Of all the poems in the Tao Te Ching, this one probably is the most controversial. There is reference to a Chinese emperor who killed thousands of his subjects through interpreting this poem in a literal manner. So, it's easy to see why people often "tiptoe" around what it is saying.

After reading Poem Five to a friend, he responded with, "I don't think much of this philosophy." Initially the poem appears to contradict the overall contents of the Tao Te Ching. In fact, the problems that have plagued the Tao Te Ching over the years have come from some sections, such as this one, which seem offensive or which seem to contradict other parts of the book. In Poem Ten, for example (Please refer to Poem Ten and 10 in the book), how can a wise ruler, a spiritual person, "love humanity and govern the country" and at the same time be cold-hearted and ruthless? As an explanation, I have heard that heaven and earth do not take sides—that the sage is impartial: that heaven and earth are indifferent and the sage is also indifferent. All these explanations fall short; in fact, Lao Tzu says exactly what he means, but you have to dig deeply into what he's implying.

What Lao Tzu teaches can be seen in a couple of ways. First, from redefining the terminology:

5

Soul and entity are without heart.
They use things for their own ends.
The wise ruler is without heart.
He uses kinship for his own ends.

The space between soul and entity
resembles breathing apparatus.
Empty and yet through constant use it doesn't collapse.
The more you push it the more it supplies.
In the pursuit of artificial learning,
what's really you is weighted down
with too many facts.
Stay in the center and become the one who truly cares.

Heaven and earth are a bit distant. Redefining the terms with soul and entity comes closer to home.

Another method is in following the thread which travels through various themes of a few other poems. By looking at the first few lines of Poem 10 one can pick up the thread running through both versions of Poems Five and Ten. Poem 10: "Bearing with the physical and spiritual forces that play tug of war in your soul, can you unify yourself in the Tao?"

Here Lao Tzu is stating that there is an internal struggle between spirit and body, and he is saying in Poem Five that heaven has its own uses for the people and that earth has its own uses for the people. The spirit has its thought-people, and the body has its thought-people. And so, what is the underlying message in Poem Five?

The message states emphatically that humanity must have a new image of itself. We must no longer be manipulated by the forces of heaven and earth, spirit and body, male and female, light and darkness. Somehow, we must find a way to transcend the duality of the world and bring ourselves to a complete wholeness. How do we accomplish this? Poem Five says, "The wise person is not humane and perceives the people as straw dogs." Just as people have been treated ruthlessly from being manipulated by heaven and earth, so must the true ruler manipulate the mixture of thoughts coming from soul and entity. In other words, we must find a way to balance these two forces (yin and yang), wield true power while identifying ourselves with the eternal Tao once again. The poem also points to a certain amount of selfishness or self-preservation necessary for survival in life. Either we have our own uses for the people (thoughts) or we are used slavishly by opposing forces from within ourselves.

Now, admittedly, by looking at Poem Five in and of itself—well, things don't look too good. However, when you read some of the other poems, how can a leader, "In ruling the country and loving the people" (Poem 10) or how can the wise person be good to those who are good and good to those who are bad (Poem Forty-Nine)? Clearly, there is something going on in Poem Five that seems to contradict just about everything else in the Tao Te Ching. The question is why? What point is Lao Tzu trying to make here?

First, he's telling us that the outer world, the physical universe is a dangerous place to live in. Life can be a struggle; nature can be quite cruel. There is the inevitable probability of earthquakes, exploding volcanoes, floods, tornadoes and wandering asteroids that can strike our vulnerable planet at any time. Then there are billions upon billions of hungry self-centered creatures. There are birds and bees, tigers and trees, there are humans, and virtually everyone wants "a piece of the action." Everyone who has a body has their own self-interest and their own hungers that need to be fulfilled.

Let me give a different example: if you notice that above the front door of your house there's a wasp's nest, you may at first choose to go through the back door of your house for a time but the question is: how long will you be willing to go through the back door? Do you give up the front area of your house to a group of wasps or in self-defense do you kill the wasps or remove them? What are your limitations and what are your boundaries? How big or small is your sphere of influence on the world going to be? How large is your ego? What is your belief system? And of course, this is taking into account that other poems in the Tao Te Ching are talking about forgiveness and love. Yet, no matter how hard we try, there are going to be times when a certain amount of self-defense is unavoidable. Also, it's entirely possible that in opening your front door and stepping outside, you may have inadvertently killed some tiny creatures that you didn't even notice. This is what the Tao Te Ching is talking about.

Poem Five tells us that at times everyone is so caught up with self and selfishness that it seems that there is no caring going on in the world. "Straw dogs" were sacrificial items that were thrown away after they were used. This may be difficult to grasp but this poem is actually saying something similar to what Rabbi Hillel said, "If I am not for myself, then who will be for me? If I am not for others, what am I? If not now, when?"

The poem states there's a space between heaven and earth and Lao Tzu is telling us that we are the ones who can fill the space. We are the ones who can bring caring into an uncaring world. We are the ones who can develop a special "heart" of compassion. That's because we are the ones who are to become what humans were truly meant to be.

Tao Te Ching—viii

A Plain Uncut Block of Wood

I have said that my interpretations would consist of a "somewhat orthodox" version and a more liberal one. Since I don't speak or write Chinese, I decided to not try to be totally consistent in every instance. For example, one translation might use the word "virtue" over and over. In my interpretations, I might use virtue in one poem but I will also use the word goodness or purity in place of the word virtue in other poems.

Another example of this can be found in Poem Fifteen. "A plain uncut block of wood" is sited. In other works it's called "uncarved wood" or "an uncarved block." In my versions after the fifteenth poem, it's referred to as "the uncut form" and "uncarved form."

What is this wood or "uncut form" and in practical terms, how can we use this form? When we identify with the uncut form (mother-father), it represents going back to the formless state and it also represents something more. The uncut form is the whole of creation before embodiment and its initial totality remains after it takes shape and becomes manifest. For humanity, it can be a refuge, a haven—for if we can lay our troubled, divided natures on this uncut form, then we gain the power to change the things in our lives that we have never been able to deal with before (see Poem 62). By realizing that we are a part of a "greater whole," we gain our freedom—for within the uncut form there is "space" for all of us. We are able to retain our individualities and still be a part of the total oneness. That is the magnificent beauty of the Tao.

The Spiritual Person

The most important factor in gaining our freedom deals with the wise person/wise ruler. Poem Two is the first that speaks about the "wise person." In most translations, the wise person is called "the sage." In my versions, the sage is usually called "the wise person" or "the spiritual person" or "the superior leader." Who is this spiritual person or superior leader? In Poem Seventeen it says, "The superior ruler is hardly noticed by the people."

Here Lao Tzu is saying that there is a spiritual person who resides in each one of us. The spiritual person is the true heart (self) in all hearts (see Poem Forty-Nine). The spiritual person is a protector, a guide, a teacher, and yes, an emancipator. He (male wedded to female and beyond both) is in each of us but is very difficult to discern. He is "elusive, mysterious" (Poem 17). He will not be found completely in a personal teacher or "guru." In fact, Poems Eighteen and Nineteen warn us against following a lie. Ultimately, this lie tells us not to believe in our own true nature. It builds up the outer and belittles the inner. As time passes, we lose the ability to come into contact with our inner self, our inner nature. We rely more on the outer world than our own "spiritual person" inside us.

How To Approach the Two Interpretations

What I have attempted to do in my book is to give you, the reader, a means to better perceive what each poem is saying. With two versions for every poem, you should acquire a more complete understanding.

Before you begin reading the poems, it's important to note that a "somewhat orthodox" version will always be on your left. The poems on the right side of the book are usually more poetic. The second interpretations were not written as explanations for the first. Rather, the second versions simplify, redefine, or expand on the first version. As a general rule, you will be able to compare both interpretations almost word for word. There are, however, a few poems where this cannot be done.

To the Female Reader

Let me say this: just because certain pronouns have been used doesn't mean that the Tao Te Ching should be considered an exclusive club for males. In fact, in the physical world, at this very instant, a spiritual person can just as easily find herself in female form. So please forgive me for being a bit biased. It just doesn't flow well when you have some poems using "he" and others using "she." And to totally exclude gender doesn't quite feel right either.

In my opinion, whether you're a man or woman, you are equally welcomed by the Tao, and you both share "equal opportunity" in your quest for enlightenment.

The Idea Behind the Illustrations

I began each drawing by meditating and concentrating on themes in the Tao Te Ching. I produced twenty-five large drawings; next, I photographed five to twelve portions from each large drawing which became the illustrations for each poem. The concept is that if each large drawing has the "spirit" of the Tao as portrayed in the Tao Te Ching, then the parts have meaning for each of the eighty-one poems. To match just the right portion with the appropriate poems, I constantly used the I-Ching. With the I-Ching, I was able to test and verify that the poems and the images convey the mystery, wonder and truth inherent in the Tao Te Ching.

About two or three years after I produced the drawings and matched them with the poems, I was reading a book on Taoism. The book explained that Lao Tzu had been described as having large ears and no orifices, no mouth or openings.

This bit of information almost knocked me over because I had always wondered if I had used the proper image for the first poem of the book: it shows Lao Tzu as having a mouth that looked like it had been closed with a zipper and with large ears and closed eyes.

That said, hopefully, from your reading and comparing each pair of poems and images, you will "taste the taste of the tasteless," that is—you will learn what cannot be "imparted or taught." I wish you a successful journey:

The Tao is the way—the way a path.
The path is a road.
The road is vast.
Walk the road that is a path.
Follow the path that is the way.
Live the life that is vast.

RMJ

Tao Te Ching
Lao Tzu

An Intuitive Interpretation by Robert M. Jankel

One

The Tao that can be spoken of
is not the eternal Tao.
The name that can be named
is not an eternal name.
That which cannot be named is the beginning
of heaven and earth.
The named is the mother of the ten thousand beings.
Therefore, persistently eliminate your desires
if you wish to see its mysteries,
but persistently hold to your desires
if you wish to see its manifestations.
These two have the same source and differ in name only.
This is a mystery in a mystery,
the gateway to the deepest mystery.

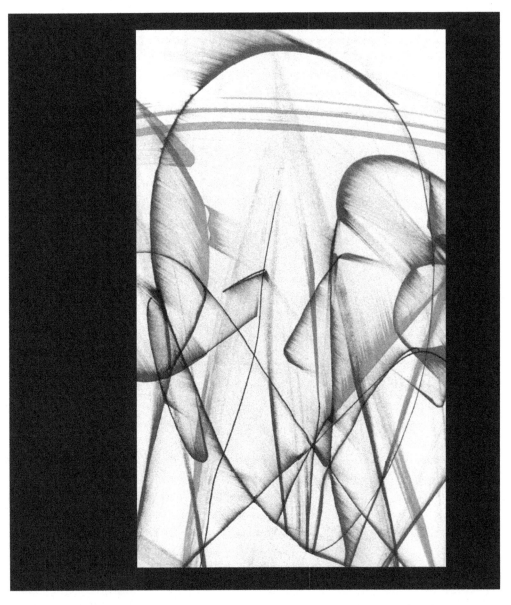

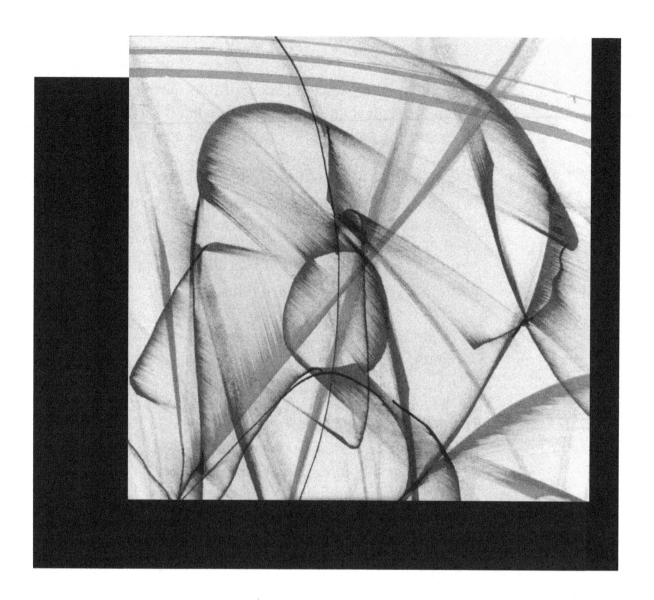

<u>1</u>

The way that can be described is not an enduring way.
The word once spoken is not an enduring word.

An undefined womb is the origin of soul and entity.
A defined womb is the mother of all intelligence.
Therefore, remain in the womb without your drives
if you want to observe its inner unity
but in leaving the womb hold to your drives
if you want to observe its outer differences.
These two come from the same place
and differ in word only.
This is the deepest mystery,
the opening to the most profound secret.

Two

The people recognize the beautiful for beautiful
only through acknowledgment of what is repulsive.
The people recognize the good from knowing what is bad.

So something and nothing fashion each other.
Difficult and easy bring out the best in each other.
Long and short differentiate each other.
High and low are attracted to each other.
Sound and silence are in accord with each other.
Front and back pursue each other.

Therefore, a wise person keeps still and instructs
others in the silent way.

The ten thousand beings come and go forever,
and it never asks for acknowledgment.
It brings life yet renounces any possessions.
It helps us all but never asks to be obliged.
It does the job without taking credit.
Hence, its essence is beyond value.

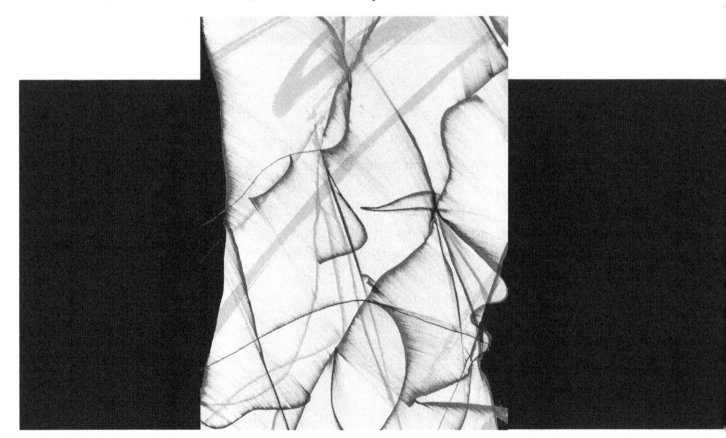

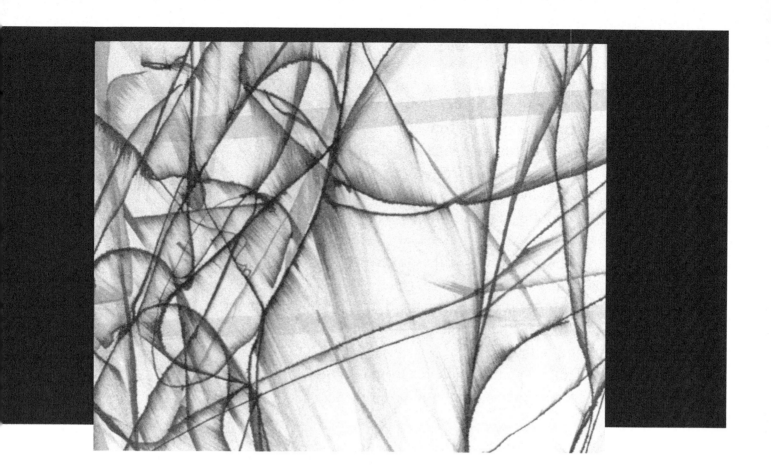

2

When everyone sees something as being attractive,
this already states their acceptance of what is unattractive.
When everyone agrees on something as being virtuous,
this already states their acceptance of what is unvirtuous.

Definition and the undefined create,
toil and rest complete,
gain and loss compare,
light and darkness embrace,
thunder and stillness harmonize,
winners and losers give chase,
these are the extremes.

Thus, the spiritual person teaches with the Tao of silence.
In the Tao, life eternally unfolds and brings forth
without possessiveness.
In the Tao, everything is brought to completion
without being aware of it.
It is because it never asks for gratitude
that it deserves immeasurable praise.

Three

Not being enchanted by those with talent
keeps the people from strife.
Not coveting and amassing precious things
discourages thievery.
Not showing off desirable things circumvents
a chaotic state of mind.

Therefore, a wise ruler governs by emptying
minds and filling stomachs.
He reduces distinctions and makes bones stronger.
He keeps the people unknowing
and without desire.
This prevents the clever from acting.
Don't move and a basic order prevails.

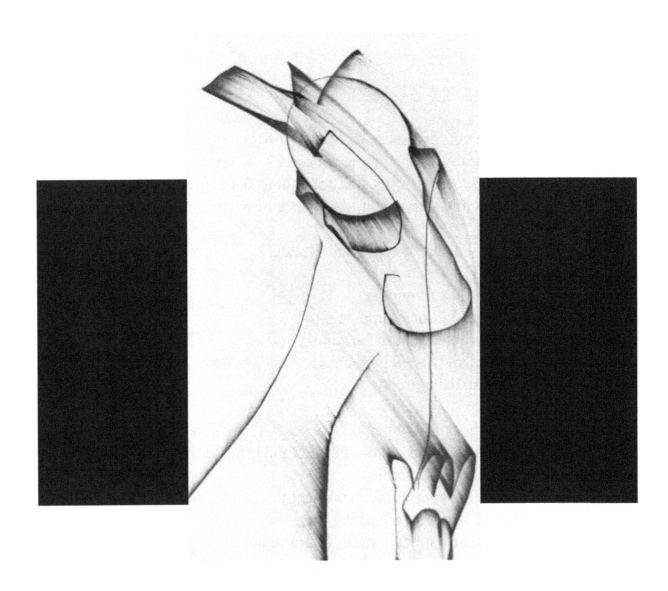

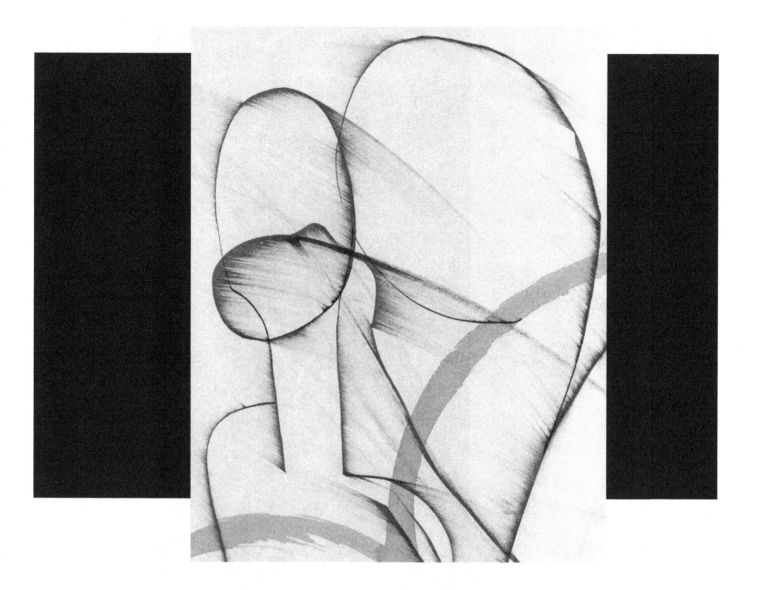

3

By not raising up the gifted, you prevent envy.
By not craving valuable things, you prevent piracy.
By not making a show of your treasured things,
you prevent discontent.

Thus, a spiritual leader empties the heart
and fills the gut,
weakens desires and builds strong frames.
He brings people back to a state of innocence
by curbing ambition
and guiding them away from artificial learning.
This prevents the devious from taking action.
By not acting, everyone finds his place.

Four

Tao is like an empty bowl.
Use it, it's an endless source.
Vast, it is the provider of life
to the ten thousand beings.
Make smooth the sharpness.
Untie the knots.
Decrease the glare.
Travel the tried and true and merge with the dust.
For it's difficult to see but, oh, is it there!
I don't know where it comes from.
It stands before the names of God.

4

The way is a swirling-whirling nothingness.
Employ it, it will not run out.
Fathomless, it is the source of all things.

Bend your unyieldingness.
End your confusion.
Dim your brightness.
Continually use the path
that has brought you your success.
Like deep water it seems to remain.
I barely perceive of its existence.
I don't know what branch it came from.
It seems to have pre-dated God.

Five

Heaven and earth are not humane
and perceive the ten thousand beings as straw dogs.
The wise person is not humane
and perceives the people as straw dogs.

It's that space between heaven and earth,
isn't it like a bellows,
empty—yet not devoid of life.
Move it back and forth and never stop using it.
Talk too much and you become exhausted.
Better hold tightly to what you already have within.

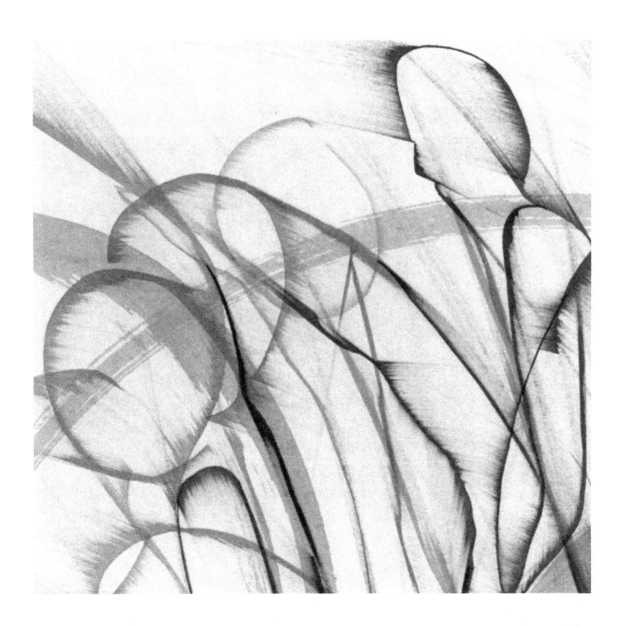

5

Soul and entity are without heart.
They use things for their own ends.
The wise ruler is without heart.
He uses kinship for his own ends.

The space between soul and entity
resembles breathing apparatus.
Empty and yet through constant use it doesn't collapse.
The more you push it the more it supplies.
In the pursuit of artificial learning,
what's really you is weighted down
with too many facts.
Stay in the center and become the one who truly cares.

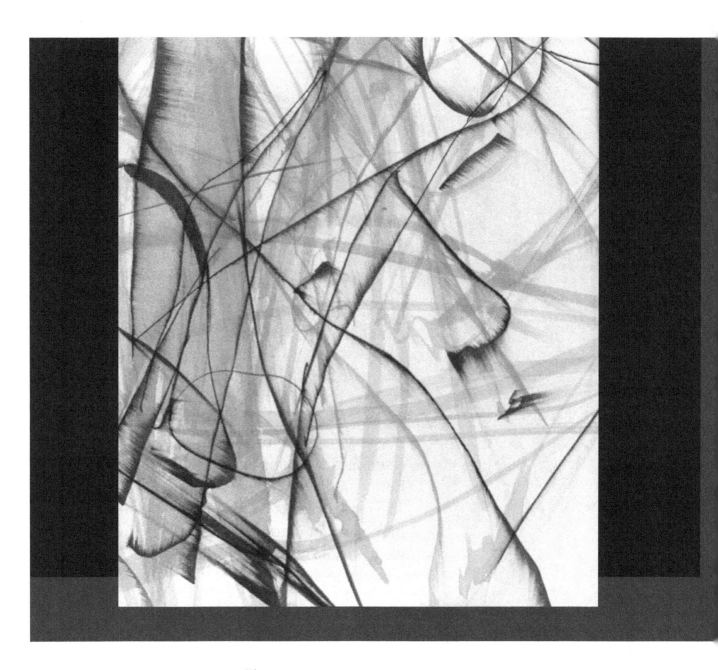

Six

The valley and the spirit live forever.
It is the venerable mother.
Her gateway is the source of heaven and earth.
Barely discernible, she seems to be there.
Cling to her, she never dies.

6

The spirit in the womb never dies.
She's called the mysterious female
whose way is the origin of yang and yin.
A shadow and a blur, is she really there?
Use her, for she endlessly perpetuates
without effort.

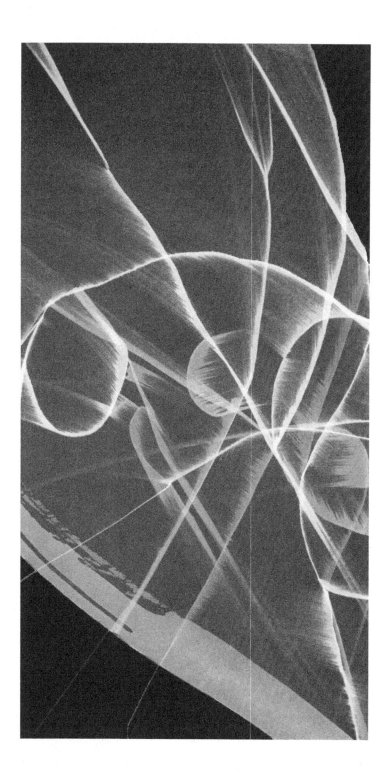

Seven

Heaven and Earth remain.
They remain
because they choose not to live for themselves.
That is why they remain.
A wise person has no need to be first.
Therefore, he cannot lose.
It is because he doesn't hold himself as someone
of importance.
Acting without thought of self, he insures success.

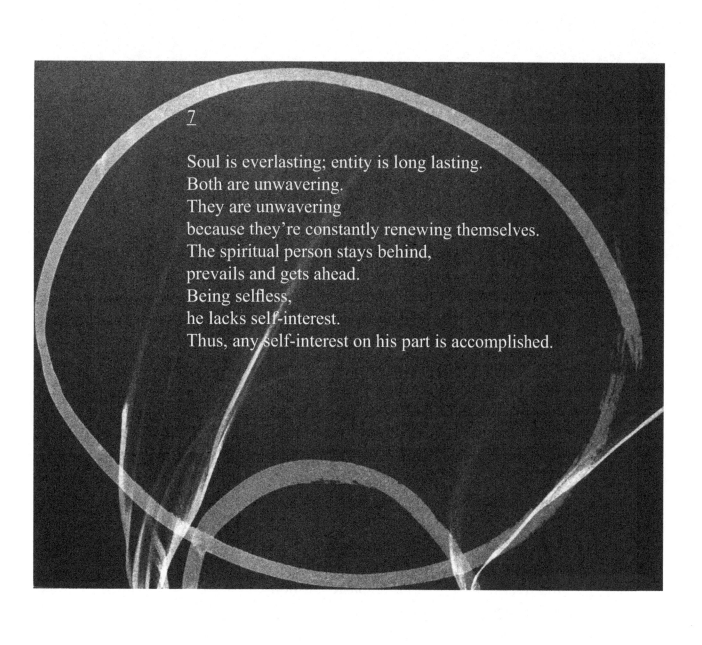

7

Soul is everlasting; entity is long lasting.
Both are unwavering.
They are unwavering
because they're constantly renewing themselves.
The spiritual person stays behind,
prevails and gets ahead.
Being selfless,
he lacks self-interest.
Thus, any self-interest on his part is accomplished.

Eight

Water is akin to the highest good.
Water sustains the ten thousand beings
without striving against them.
Water stays in places all creatures reject.
In this way, water is like the Tao.

In a house, look for the proper location.
In thinking, dwell on the profound.
In choosing a friend, look for a kind heart.
In speech, be true to yourself.
In governing, maintain the basic harmony.
In business, employ competence.
In making your move, bide your time.
When you don't strive, you go unmarked.

8

Soft and weak resemble the great Tao.
Soft and weak benefit the living without struggle.
Soft and weak remain in places all men hate.
This is the path that is of the highest goodness.

In your living, bring goodness to its proper place.
In your feelings, bring goodness to the depths.
In your relating to others, bring goodness to friendship.
In your words, bring goodness to sincerity.
In your ruling, bring goodness to the system.
In your work, bring goodness to the right time and place.
Without struggling, bring goodness on your path to success.

Nine

Best to stop short than to fill to the brim.
Hone a blade too much, and it quickly
has a blunt edge.
Fill a room with gold and jade,
and it cannot be held.
To vaunt wealth and position brings misfortune
on oneself.
Rest when the job is complete.
This is heaven's way.

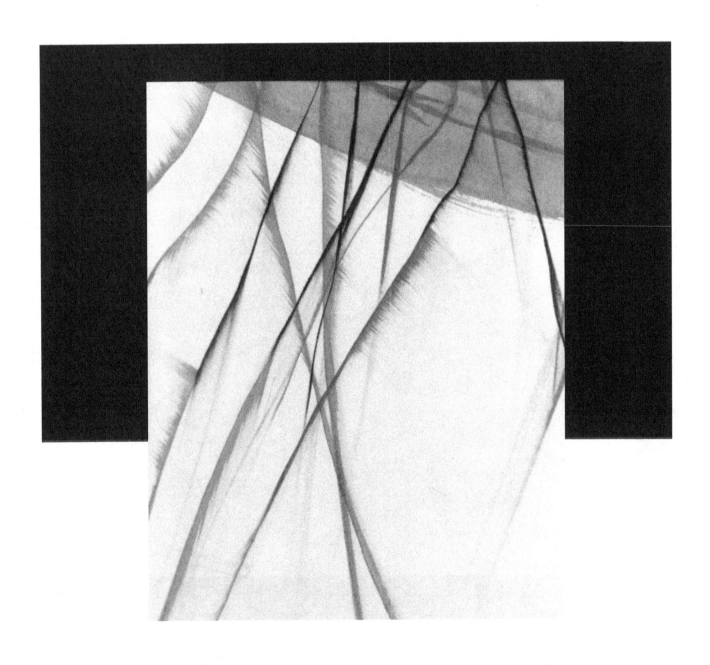

9

Possessing until it overflows,
using until it wears out,
better to have left it alone.
Fill a space with precious things,
and there will always be someone to pirate it.
Try to use wealth and power; be puffed up with pride,
this is called self-destruction.
When the work is done, it's time to relax.
This is the Tao of heaven.

Ten

With all the turmoil that goes on in your soul,
can you still hold tightly to the oneness?
Can you vitalize yourself
and be as open as a new born babe?
Can you polish the reflecting mirrors of your mind
without leaving a stain?
Can you love humanity and govern the country
without making a move?
Can you take the part of the female,
when opening and closing the gates of heaven?
Can your understanding penetrate through the heavens?
Are you able to not know yourself?

The way is like a parent to the living.
The way brings life without trying to control.
The way benefits the living but doesn't ask for thanks.
The way is a sovereign who does not take dominion.
This is called the mysterious goodness.

10

Bearing with the physical and the spiritual forces
that play tug of war in your soul,
can you unify yourself in the Tao?
In keeping your energy in balance,
in order to be soft and weak,
can you renew yourself?
In cleansing your intuitive seeing,
can you be without fault?
In ruling the country and loving the people,
can you lead them without being crafty?
In opening and closing the gates of your spirit,
can you take the female role of stillness?
In detecting the hidden universe
with the clarity of your vision, can you be still?

Conceiving
but not possessing,
benefiting
but not asking for anything in return,
governing
but not managing,
these are the secrets of goodness.

Eleven

Thirty spokes join the center of the hub.
Utilize the void within to fulfill your aspirations,
and set about driving the cart.
Form the clay into a jar.
Utilize the void within to fulfill your desires,
and gain the use of the jar.
Carve doors and windows to form a room.
Utilize the void within to fulfill your dreams,
and obtain the use of the room.
Thus, we acquire substance, but the use of substance
comes from the void.

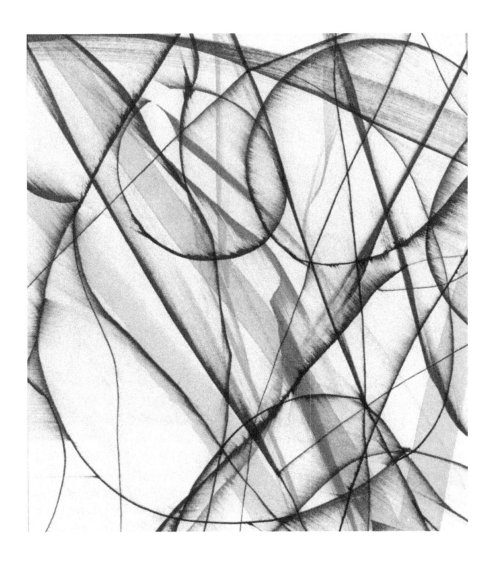

11

Resembling spokes converging on a hub of a wheel,
we become a group of unique parts
through the use of the spirit
and holding to the greater w-hole.
Resembling the shaping of clay pots,
we perfect ourselves
through the use of the spirit
and holding to the greater w-hole.
Resembling the carving of doors and windows,
we build shelters for ourselves
through the use of the spirit
and holding to the greater w-hole.

Thus, in order to complete itself,
all life must follow the spirit
through the use of holding to the greater w-hole.

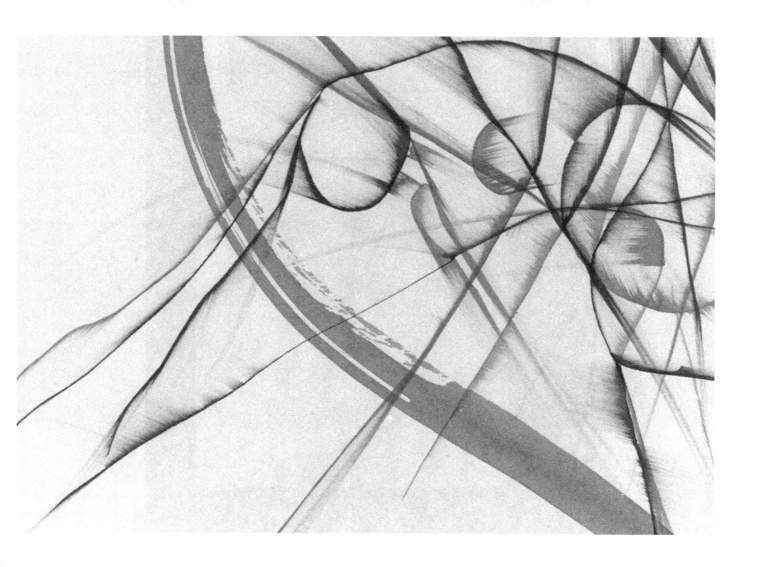

Twelve

The five colors unsettle the eye.
The five chords muffle the ear.
The five flavors confuse the tongue.
The ride and the hunt drive the headstrong wild.
The want of precious things impedes his progress.
Thus, a wise person puts no stock in what he sees
but always satisfies basic needs.
He chooses the one and discards the other.

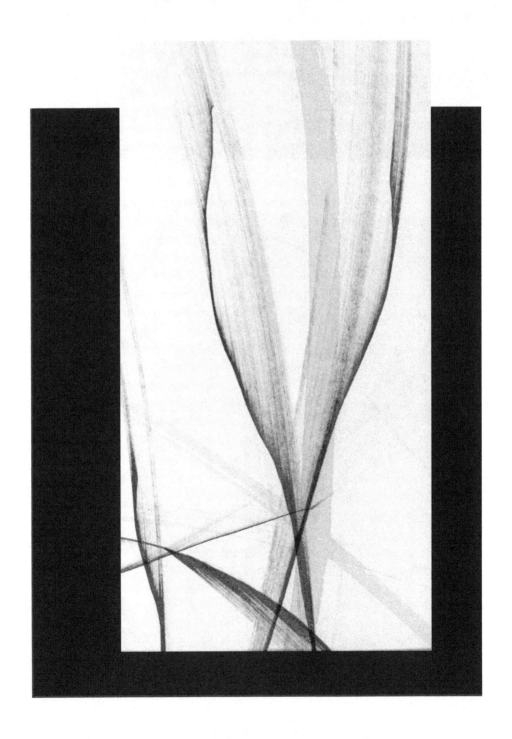

12

The five colors intoxicate the eye.
The five tones absorb the ear.
The five flavors starve the taste buds.
The hungering for one another drive men and women
to a frenzy.
The craving for more valuable things
is a stumbling block to moving forward.
Therefore, a spiritual person overlooks the dazzling
and satisfies innate necessities.
He throws away the one and takes the other.

<u>Thirteen</u>

Accept that to be honored or disgraced is a shocking thing.
What does this mean?
It means I must learn to cherish the great afflictions
of having a body (self).
What do I mean when I say,
accept that to be honored or disgraced is a shocking thing?
When I'm honored I become high about it.
When I'm disgraced I become depressed about it,
and in each situation there is the element of shock.
Therefore, it means I must learn to cherish
the great afflictions of having this body.

So, the problem is that I have this body (self).
When I'm no longer in this body, where's the problem?

Therefore, I must always begin with my own person (body-self)
before I can relate to other persons.
Then I can become fit to rule an empire.
First, I must love my own self (body)
before I bring love and government into a world of other persons.

13

Resembling characters in a drama,
sometimes we receive the role of the fortunate.
Sometimes we receive the role of the unfortunate.
What I seek and what I run from
are the cause of much bewilderment.
What does this mean?
It means I must learn
to deal with two equally difficult situations.
I am bewildered because
when I'm alive I am separate from others.
When I'm no longer alive to that separateness,
how then can I remain bewildered?
Therefore,
he who can become one with all others
can be trusted to govern the world.
He who loves the world,
as if everyone were his own offspring,
can be trusted to care for the world.

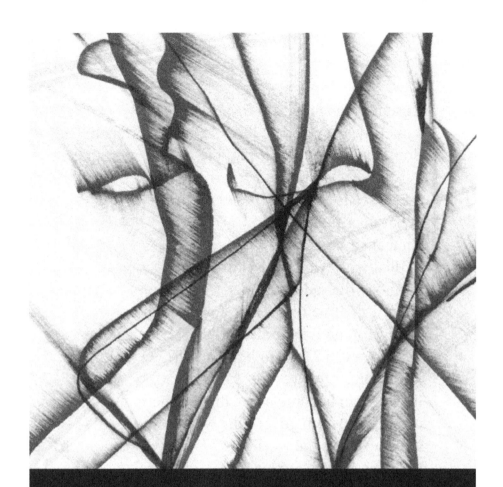

Fourteen

Can't be seen, it's called non-existent.
Can't be heard, it's called subtle.
Can't be touched, it's called minute.
Since the three cannot be examined,
they're joined together as one.
From the top there is no glare.
From below it's plainly manifest.
Barely discernible, it goes unnamed
and returns to the nothingness.
Call this the form without form,
the immaterial image.
Call this the mysterious and obscure.
From the front, you can't see where it begins.
From behind, you can't see where it ends.
So follow the ancient way
to gain control of your life in the present.
This knack for knowing archaic origins,
call this the path traveling through the way.

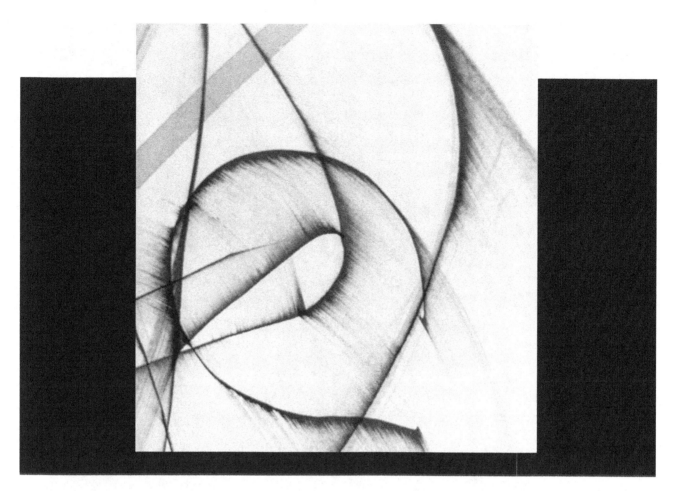

14

Look for it but you won't see it;
it's called the unperceived.
Listen for it but you won't hear it;
it's called the inaudible.
Grope for it but you won't touch it;
it's called the tiny.
Because you cannot pull these three apart,
they are taken as the oneness.
Its head is not full of preconceived ideas.
Its heart is not full of ignorance.
It is unused, uncared-for and remains the undefined.
It revolves around the formless.
This is called defining without using words,
seeing a form without using your eyes,
making clothing for the secret and obscure.
Approach its face, you won't see its beginning.
Follow it from behind, you won't see its ending.
Return to the formless
to resolve your problems of today.
This is a thread going through the way.

Fifteen

Long ago, those who were well-informed
of the way were subtle, mystically aware and penetrating.
Going so deep, they defied human understanding.
We can only try to bridge the gap.
What were they really like?
Careful, like someone crossing a river in winter.
Reserved, like a first time guest.
Cautious, like someone who has a reason
to suspect his neighbors.
Slowly changing, like melting ice.
Uncomplicated, like a plain uncut block of wood.
They were like an empty valley—like dark muddy water.

Who can start off being murky and opaque
and little by little become clear and translucent?
Who can be totally still but slowly stirring
know the right moment in which to move?
That is the person who clings to the way.
That is the person who doesn't crave being full,
and because he is not full,
he can grow old without the need to renew.

In ancient times, those who were educated in the way
could penetrate the most hidden mysteries.
They were so profound that they could not be defined.
Because of this,
we can only attempt to describe them.
Attentive, as though meeting grave danger; on guard,
as though meeting the unexpected.
Suspecting, as though meeting thieves; taking their time,
as though they had forever to see it all.

Coming together to form a great w-hole-ness,
willing to be enslaved and entombed for the good of all,
they resembled a barren womb
that starts off being dark but ends up full of light.

Who is it that can slowly go
from knowing nothing to knowledge and light?
Who is it that can, through stillness,
penetrate the darkness and find life?
He who does not fill himself full of static ideas,
he who always remains empty and open to new ideas
revives the old and brings new life.

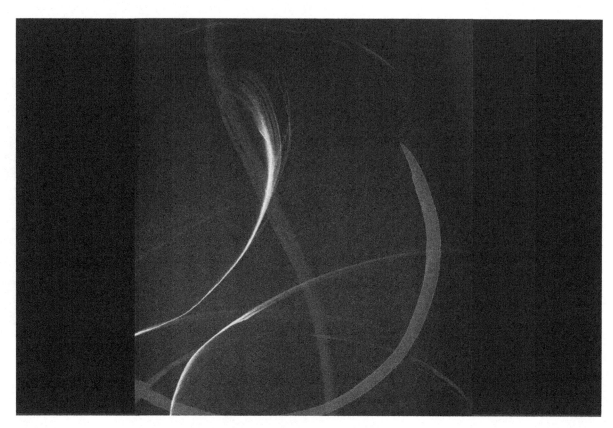

Sixteen

I go to the limit to reach emptiness
and cling to the stillness.
As the ten thousand beings make their ascension,
I'm there watching their return.
Countless creatures go back to their source.
Going back to the source is stillness.
Going back to the source is a return to my destiny.
Returning to my destiny implies the attainment of the constant.
Acquiring the constant leads to enlightenment.
Not knowing the constant leads to an attraction to violence.
First, attain the constant; then you can be all-inclusive,
and everything you do leads you to moderation.
Moderation leads to dominion of oneself (nobility).
Dominion of oneself (nobility)
leads to heaven (kingship).
Heaven (kingship) carries you to the Tao.
The Tao is eternal.
In the Tao, there is no longer fear of harm.

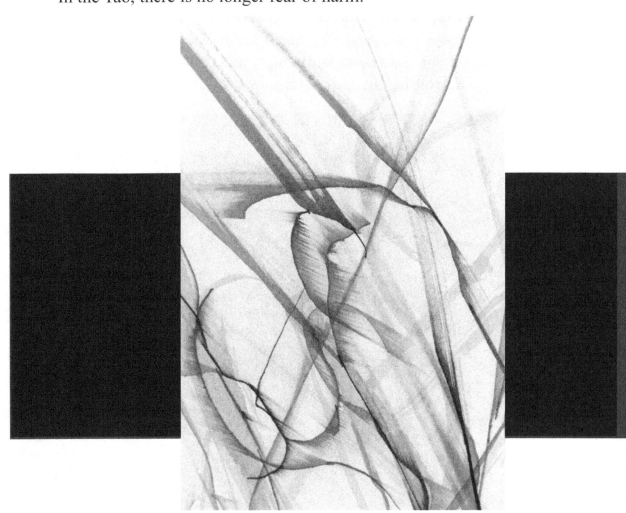

16

I work at being void of all things
and achieve self-sufficiency.
As the life forces rise up in unison,
I'm breathing slowly in and out, waiting for their return.
Resembling plants,
or a tree going through the body,
all my thoughts return to their roots.
Returning to my roots is restfulness.
Returning to my roots is returning to my allotted home.
Returning to my allotted home brings permanence.
Attaining permanence brings a sense of belonging to my life.
Not knowing permanence
is to always hunger for those things that I cannot attain.

Knowing permanence leads to self-mastery.
Self-mastery leads to self-discovery.
Self-discovery puts me on the way.

Seventeen

The superior ruler is hardly noticed by his people.
Then there is the ruler the people acknowledge
with love and gratitude.
Then there is the one they fear and despise.
Then there is the one that everybody pushes around.
When belief isn't strong enough,
there is a lack of faith.

Reluctantly he speaks and, when he does,
he weighs each word.
As the task is complete,
everyone says it happened naturally.

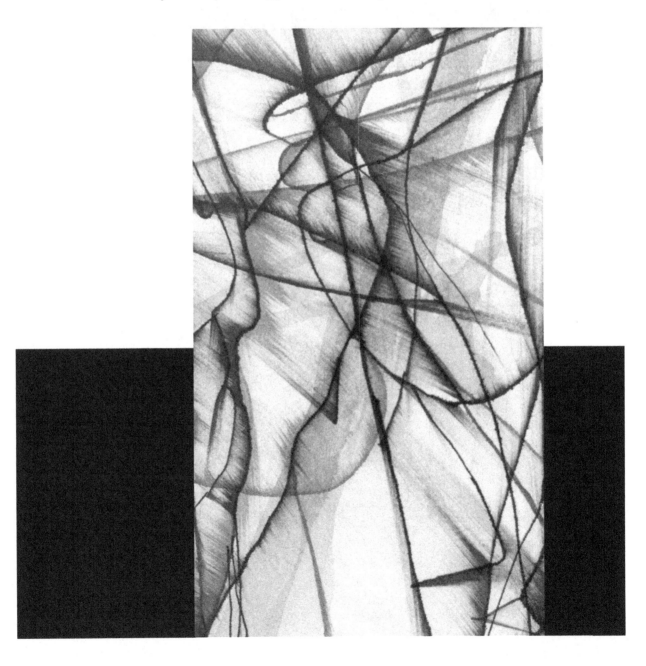

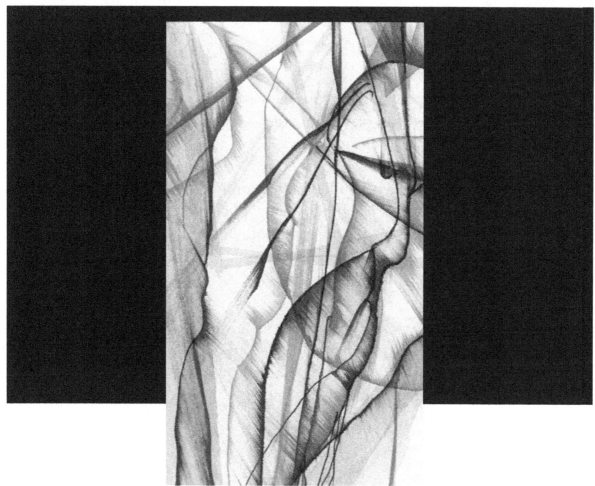

17

The greatest of leaders relies wholeheartedly on the Tao
and remains elusive, mysterious,
unknown and the protector of the people.
Then comes the leader who knows of the Tao
but whose charismatic personality sometimes blocks the way.
He is loved and praised by the people.
Then comes the leader who knows
but who uses it to serve his own selfish ends.
He is feared by the people.
Then there is the leader who doesn't know
and doesn't care.
He is hated by the people.

If a person doesn't have faith in himself,
how can he ask others to have faith in him?

He uses words only when necessary
and, when the work is done,
the people take the credit.

Eighteen

When people fail to use the vast way,
kindness and piety show themselves.
Then comes cleverness.
With that, insincerity is born.
When there is conflict in the family,
the children become loyal and obedient.
When the country is in turmoil,
devoted ministers approach.

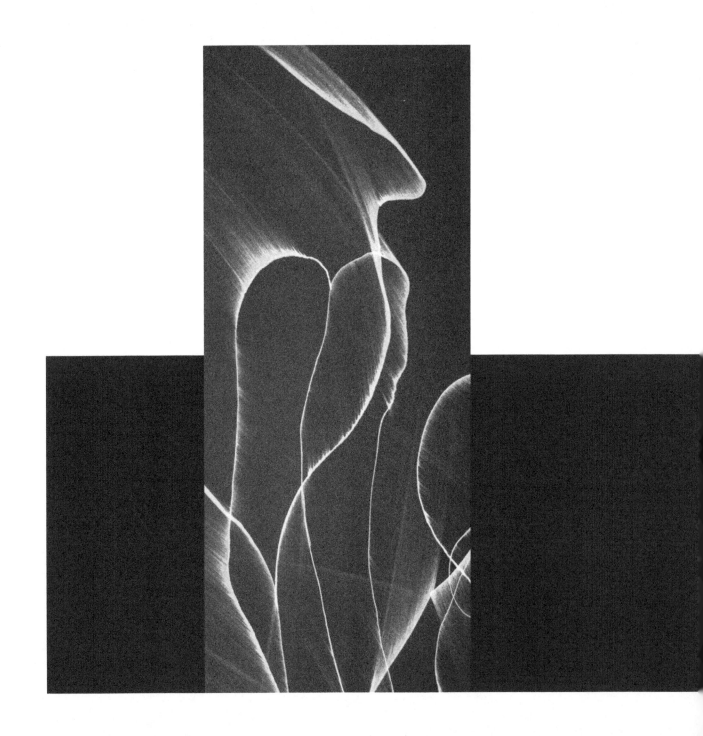

18

When Tao declines from lack of use or misuse,
do-gooders and the sanctimonious hero appear.
Next come the masters and soothsayers.
With that, a great lie is spread.
When there is rebellion within the family,
proper behavior is taught.
When there is confusion within the country,
experts and specialists vie for power.

Nineteen

Do away with sainthood. Put an end to wisdom,
and the people will thrive a thousand fold.
Do away with kindness and piety,
and the family will again be united.
Put an end to cleverness and throw out profit,
and you won't encounter thieves and thugs.
These three are flashy ornaments and will not do.
What is needed is something nourishing to cling to.

Return to simplicity; cling to the uncarved form.
Don't think of yourself as someone of importance.
Put an end to most of your desires.

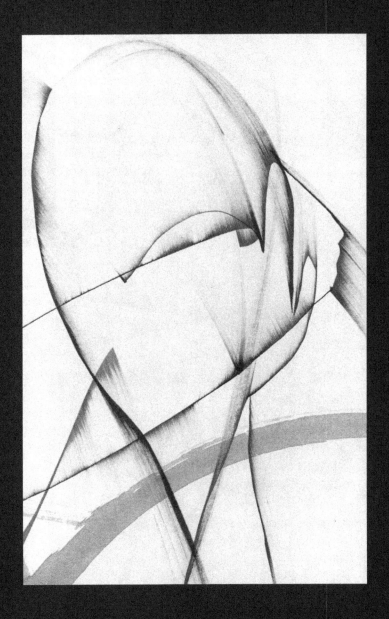

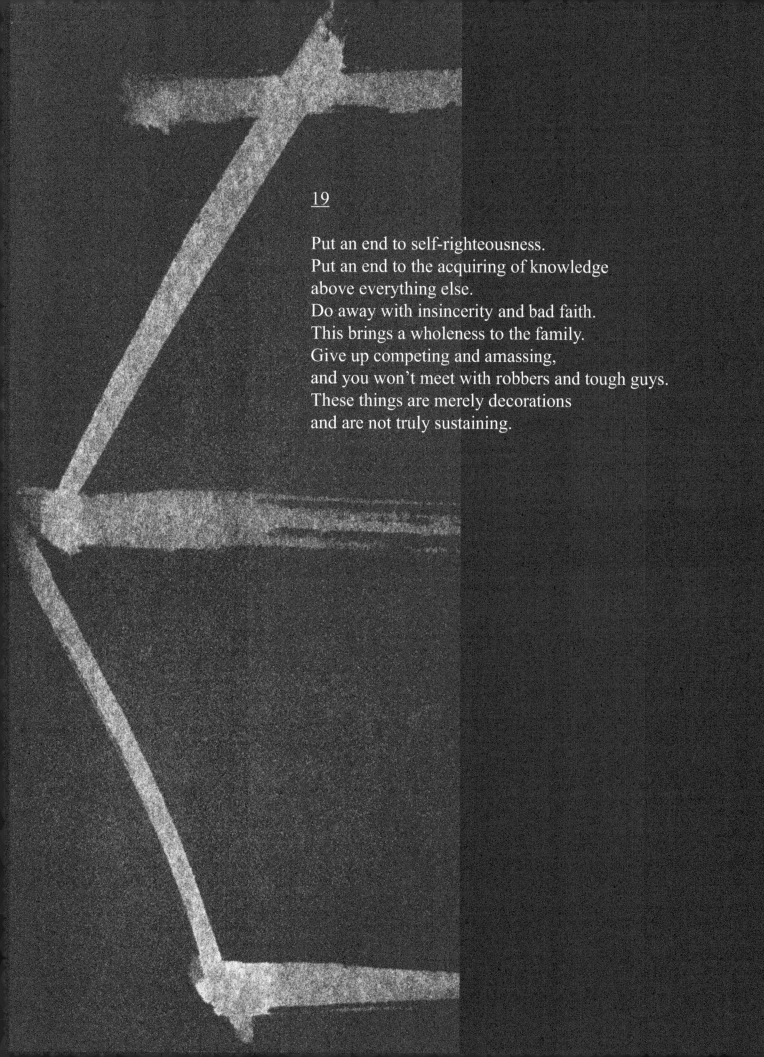

19

Put an end to self-righteousness.
Put an end to the acquiring of knowledge
above everything else.
Do away with insincerity and bad faith.
This brings a wholeness to the family.
Give up competing and amassing,
and you won't meet with robbers and tough guys.
These things are merely decorations
and are not truly sustaining.

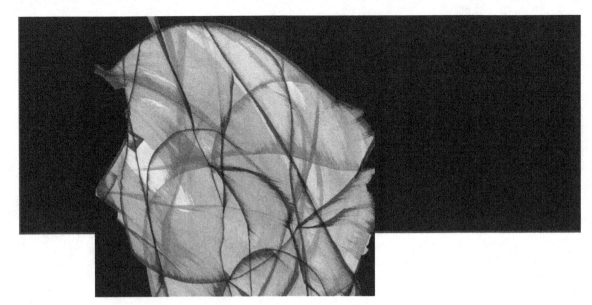

Twenty

Put away learning and anxiety vanishes.
From yes to no, what's the difference?
Between good and evil, how far apart?
What others are afraid of, must I fear, too?

Expand without reaching an end.

Everyone is joyous,
as if they had been invited to a banquet
or had gone walking through gardens
and up terraces in the spring.
I alone am unmoved and unreadable.
I'm like the baby who doesn't yet know how to smile—
Lethargic, as if I didn't have a home to go to.
The others all have more than enough.
I seem to be the only one lacking.
I look like a fool; my mind is missing.
A common man is quite clear but I'm cloudy.
A common man is awake but I'm drowsy.

Adrift on a turbulent sea,
I calmly go wherever the windstorm takes me.

The people all have a goal.
But I alone am without aim—a numskull
and a clown.
I'm not like the others.
I'm led and fed by the great mother.

Can you define the difference between yes and maybe?
Can you measure the distance between right and wrong?
Must I keep to the same line that everyone else is in?

For the universe moves in all directions and is unlimited.

Everyone is delighted to be attached to others
or to have contemplated some beautiful form.
Only me, I am confused and going in all directions.
Only me, I am like a baby too young to be affected
by outside forces, too young to see the signs.
Only me, I am noisy and aimless
as if I didn't have a home.
Everyone has abundant wealth.
Only me, I am in want.
My heart is filled with foolishness.
My mind is muddled and ignorant.
Everyone is so organized and together.
Only me, I am falling apart.
Everyone is so intelligent.
Only me, I can't get away from myself.
Persistent like waves hitting a beach,
unattached, forming and reforming,
I go with the flow of things.
Everyone has a reason for existence.
Only me, I don't know which direction to go.
Only me, I am different from others.
I am sustained by the great mother.

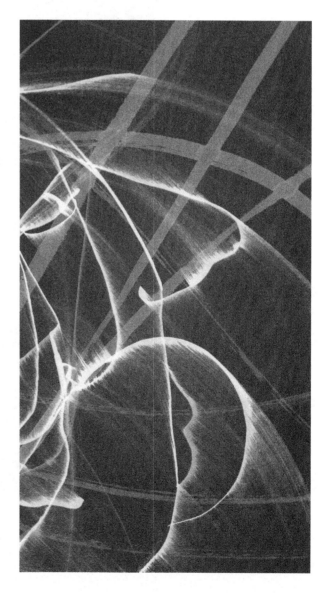

Twenty-One

In every act the wise person follows only the way.
In describing the way—it's like this:
mysterious and barely visible,
but look within, and there's a clear picture (image).
Barely visible and mysterious,
but look within, and there's meaning (substance).
Dark and murky,
but look within, there's essence (life).
This essence is quite real—look within—it can be examined.
From this moment back to the beginning of time,
its power (name) has never declined.

He serves as a way for knowing
and identifying the source.
How do I know this—because of this.

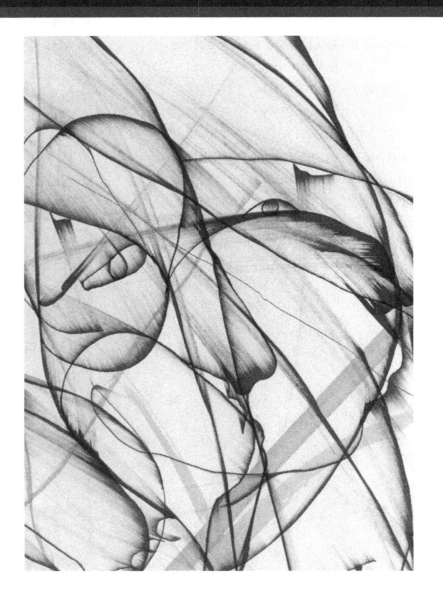

21

All the energy from life eternally follows the Tao.

The Tao goes from utter stillness to life
secretly in dim light.

For its images are dark and obscure.
So deep and obscure but within is a parent.
This parent is like a father to the living.
Hold to him; you can depend on him.
From the beginning, until this very day,
we need to define the unknown
in order to get a better look at things.
How does one know this?
From one's faith in the parent of all things.

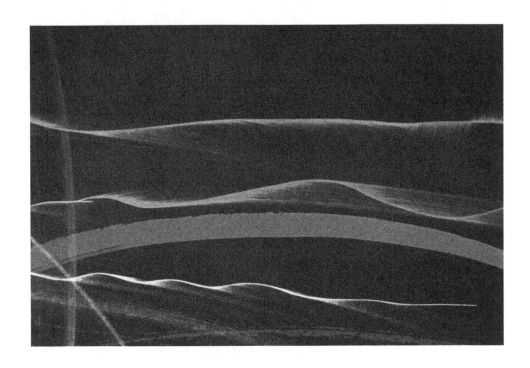

Twenty-two

Yield and you will be sustained.
Bend and you will be made straight.
Empty and you will be full (fulfilled).
Wear out and you will be made anew.
Have a little and you will be prosperous.
Have much and you will be perplexed.
Therefore, a wise person holds on to the oneness
and is an example for the world.
He chooses not to be seen and is acknowledged by all.
He doesn't see himself as perfect
and is radiantly beautiful.
He doesn't brag and is worthy of praise.
He doesn't boast and is preserved.
He doesn't strive, and there is no one
in the world who wants to strive against him.
In ancient times it was:
yield and you will be sustained.
Are these meaningless words?
Yield and be whole.

22

Be accepting and become renewed.
Be flexible and become unbreakable.
Be barren and become full.
Be weak and become strong.
Be worthless and become rich in spirit.
Be fruitful and become drained.

The spiritual person holds to form and definition
and is a pattern for the world to follow.

He remains unknown and undefined and gains great fame.
He remains flawed and shines through the darkness.
He remains unpretentious and is exalted.
He remains without pride and is prolonged.
He remains tranquil and attains peace.
In the distant past, it was
be accepting and become renewed.

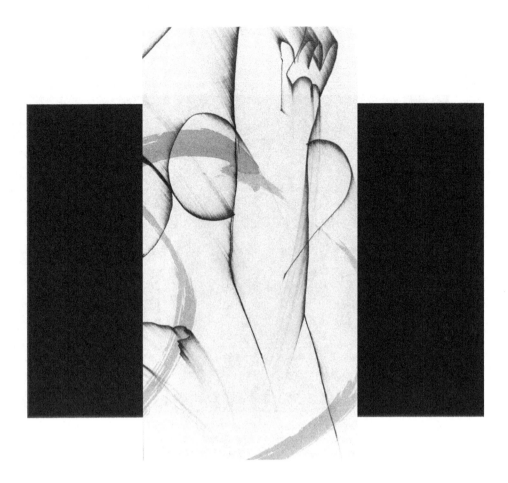

<u>Twenty-Three</u>

Not to talk too much is natural.
A strong wind won't last through the morning.
An abrupt cloudburst won't last all day.
What causes this?
Heaven and earth—yet, even heaven and earth
won't last forever.
What does this say for man?
This is the reason for my following the way.

The wise person adapts to the way.
The righteous person adapts to the righteousness.
The person of misfortune adapts to the misfortune.
The wise person who adapts to the way is welcomed
by the way.
The person who adapts to righteousness is welcomed
by the righteousness.
The person who adapts to misfortune is welcomed
by the misfortune.
When belief isn't strong enough,
there is a lack of faith.

23

To be talkative is to be wasteful.
To pursue what is impermanent is to exhaust yourself.
To live your life without the Tao is to be out of balance.
Even planets and stars have an end—
How much less your body and your creative energy?
Therefore,
to be in accord with the Tao
is to be at one with all life.
If you are in accord with the Tao,
you are at one with spiritual life.
If you are in accord with the Tao,
you are at one with physical life.

To be in accord with the Tao
is to be embraced by (the) all.

To be at one with the Tao
is to be embraced by the wealth of life.
To be at one with the Tao
is to be embraced by the poverty of life.
Without faith there is a loss of confidence.

Twenty-Four

He who stands on tiptoes cannot be balanced.
He who runs cannot slow down.
He who shows off cannot be seen.
He who is self-righteous cannot shine.
He who brags cannot be worthy of praise.
He who boasts cannot preserve.
To those traveling the way, they view these
as too much food and excess baggage.
Therefore, they must reject them wholeheartedly.

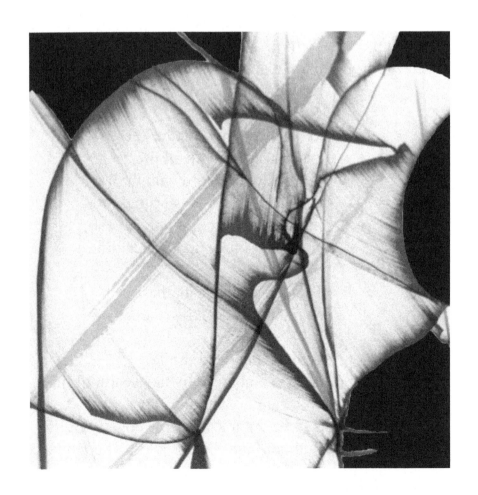

24

Standing on tiptoes, one is not stable.
In haste, one cannot walk.
Attempting to be seen, one gets lost.
Attempting to be self-important,
one becomes inconsequential.
In being an egotist, one does not endure.

Those walking in the Tao see these as too much
weight to carry
while walking on the path.

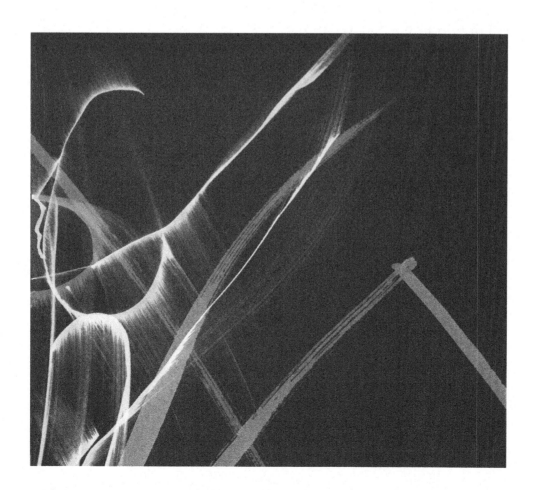

Twenty-Five

There is something perplexingly formed.
Born before heaven and earth, void and silent,
alone it stands and goes unchanged,
does the rounds and never tires.
Maybe it is the mother of ten thousand beings.
I don't know what to call it,
so I just call it the way.
For want of better words, I also call it
the renowned.
Since it's renowned, it can also be characterized
as withdrawing.
Withdrawing, it is characterized
as being a long distance away.
Having gone a long distance away, it is characterized
as returning.

Therefore, the Tao is renowned.
Heaven is renowned; earth is renowned.
The king is also renowned.
In the domain, there are four that are renowned,
and the king is one of them.
Man imitates the earth.
Earth imitates heaven.
Heaven imitates the way.
The way naturally follows the Tao.

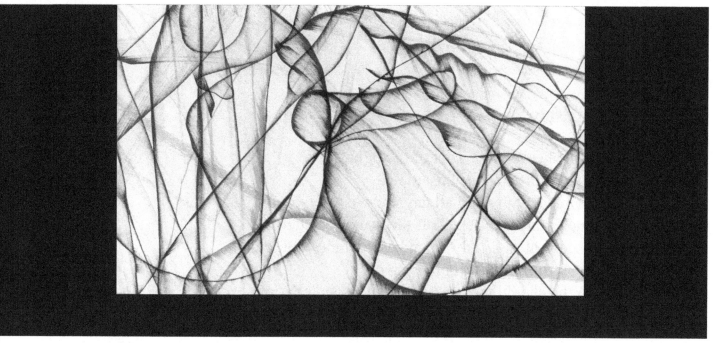

25

Before the occurrence of soul and entity,
something without shape existed.
Motionless, silent and completely whole,
alone and lonely, it is immutable.
It revolves around the formless.
It can be called the mother of all things.
I can't exactly define her, so I call her Tao.
If I am forced into giving her a name,
I will call her great.
Because she is great, she can also be described
as delving inward.
Delving inward, she can be described
as being a long way from the beginning of things.
After going on such a long journey, she can be described
as turning around.

Therefore, Tao is great.
Soul and entity are great.
The ruler is also great.
In the world, there are four that are great,
and the ruler is among them.

Man follows the body.
The body follows the spirit.
The spirit follows the way.
The way simply follows itself.

Twenty-Six

The heavy is the root of the light.
The still rules the unsettled.
Thus, in traveling all day, the wise person
never takes his eyes off the heavily loaded carts
and is at ease only when he is behind four walls
that overlook the entire region.
Why should the ruler of ten thousand chariots
belittle himself before the whole nation?
Become light and the root is lost.
Become unsettled and the ruler is lost.

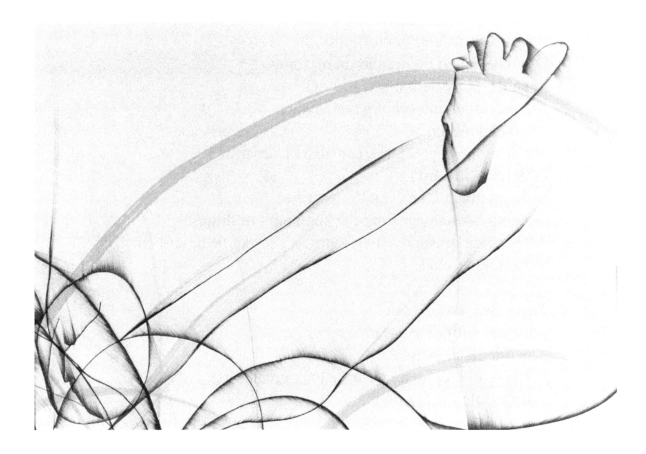

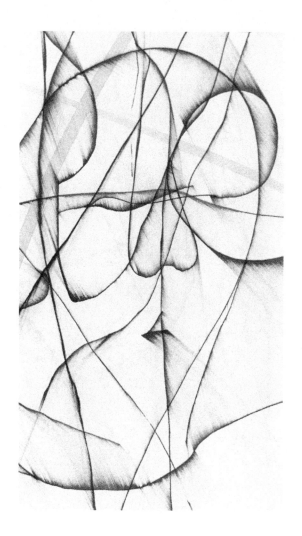

26

Earnestness came before negligence.
Tranquility controls the troubled.

Therefore, wherever the spiritual person goes,
he never strays from the important tasks at hand.
Not until every detail has been taken care of,
not until he is on high ground
and in a secure place,
does he allow himself to relax in the tranquil
recalling the many scenes.

How can someone with important duties
neglect his responsibilities?
Without earnestness you lose your composure.
Without tranquility you lose yourself.

Twenty-Seven

An excellent traveler doesn't leave wheel marks.
An excellent speaker doesn't make slips.
An excellent reckoner doesn't need an abacas.
An excellent door stopper doesn't use a lock,
but what has been closed can't be opened.
An excellent tier of knots doesn't use a cord,
but what has been tied can't be pulled apart.
Thus, the wise person has a talent
for saving people and abandons no one.
He has this talent for saving things
and abandons nothing.
This is called following your insight.
Therefore, the good man is the teacher
of a bad man.
The bad man is the substance the good works on.
If the teacher is not appreciated and valued,
and the student goes unnurtured and unloved,
chaos results no matter how clever one is.
This is called the fundamental and the mysterious.

27

The true sightseer doesn't need to move from his place.
The true speaker doesn't need to move his lips.
The true mathematician doesn't need to use a machine.
The true safe maker doesn't need to use a lock or key.
The true psychotherapist doesn't need to see his patients.
Therefore, a spiritual person is an expert
in knowing how to help others
and doesn't give up on anyone.

This is the true seeing.

Thus, one who sees should help one who cannot see.
The good should teach—
For what value is it to have knowledge
without goodness.
This only leads to great danger.
This is the inner concealment.

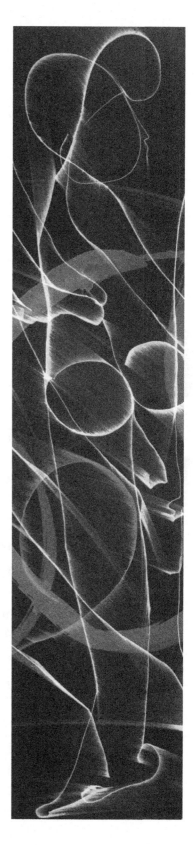

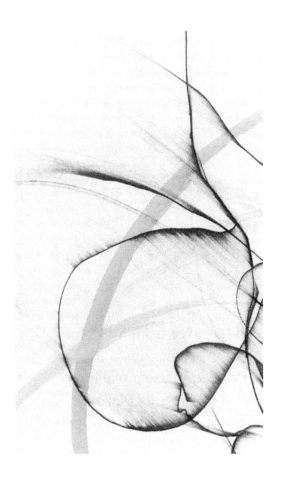

Twenty-Eight

Know the male,
but follow the role of the female.
Be like a canyon to the kingdom,
and wholeness will not desert you,
and you will go back to being childlike again.
Know the white,
but follow the role of the transgressor (black).
Be an example to the kingdom,
and wholeness will not be lacking,
and you will go back to the eternal.
Know fame but follow the role of the unknown.
Be like a valley to the kingdom,
and wholeness will be sufficient,
and you will go back to the uncut form.
Shatter the uncut form,
and the pieces (officials) try to usurp power
forcing the wise person into rulership.
Thus, the best cutter will not separate.

Have some knowledge and experience
but hold to innocence.
Like a woman with child, take good care of each person
you come into contact with.
Life will not desert you,
and you will experience the original state of innocence.
Follow the ways of goodness,
but think of yourself as being unworthy.
Like a mother with child,
let this be the pattern that the world follows,
and the world returns to its original state of innocence,
the world returns to its original state of purity.
Stay on the road to success,
but consider yourself of little importance.
Like a woman with child, take good care of each person
you come into contact with,
and you will go back to the formless.

My birth is a sign both physically and spiritually
of my being separated from my real home.
From the beginning I learn that I am separate
and different from others.

Because this is a difficult and dangerous task,
only the spiritual person can heal my divided self.
Thus, I develop my differences
but must not forget that I am a part of a greater whole.

Twenty-Nine

He who tries to take possession of the kingdom
and attempts to make improvements will never rest—
For the kingdom is a sacred receptacle
and improvements should not be made.
He who attempts to improve the kingdom devastates it.
He who tries to take possession of the kingdom
will lose it.
Thus, some things are in front and some behind.
Some breathe softly and others breathe fretfully.
Some are vigorous and others lack strength.
Some are destroyers and others are victims.
Therefore, the wise person shuns extremes,
overindulgence and pride.

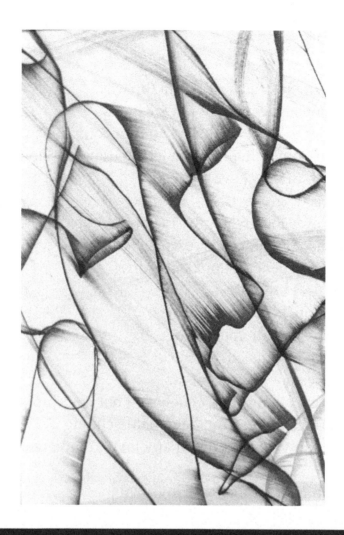

29

I have seen that whoever attempts to make the world over,
into his own image, will never succeed
because the world is something holy and spiritual.
If you arrogantly try to remake it,
you will damage it.
If you try to grasp it, it will elude you.
Some religions, some ideologies are up front
while others were meant to follow from behind.
Sometimes they're hot and sometimes cold.
Sometimes they're widely influential and sometimes not.
Sometimes they're in power and sometimes they fall.
Thus, the spiritual person takes the middle path,
keeps away from fanaticism, overzealousness,
and megalomania.

Thirty

One who instructs a ruler in the way
will not suggest a show of weapons
in order to force the kingdom into compliance.
This is something that can lead to repercussions.
Where soldiers have camped,
the weeds grow.
Wherever the great army marches, crops fail
and there are poor harvests every time.
The good general thinks in terms
of a swift victory
and a quick end to hostilities.
He does not attempt to coerce.
He brings things to an end
but does not brag or boast.
He brings things to a conclusion but isn't proud.
He brings things to its regrettable ending
out of duty and not out of any love of violence.

A man in his prime who loves violence
goes against the way.
Whoever resists the way comes to an early end.

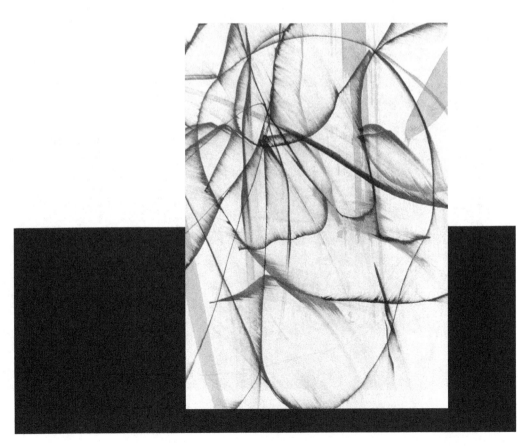

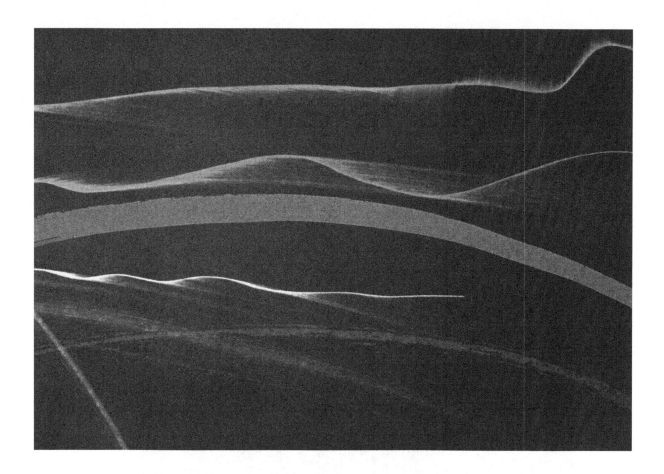

30

If you would be of service to the leader of men
through the use of the Tao,
do not try to sway the world
through aggressive and violent behavior—
this may bring some disastrous results.

Where armies meet, the land is laid waste
and the people starve.

Therefore, the wise general does not allow excessiveness,
does not resort to further violence,
does not enjoy the taking of life,
knows when to stop.

When brute force goes unrestrained,
the aging process starts.
Those who go against the Tao, die young.

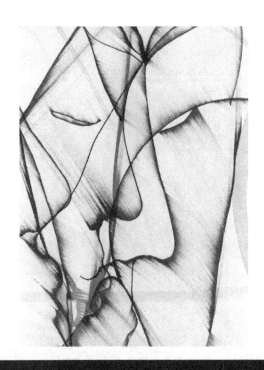

Thirty-One

Because weapons are instruments of fear,
the gentleman hates them
and does not allow their use.
The gentleman chooses the left in times of peace
and the right when going to war.
Because weapons are instruments of fear,
the gentleman does not use them.
If he is forced to use them,
he does so without taking pleasure.
For there isn't any nobility in victory,
and to glamorize it is to ennoble
the act of killing.
If he takes pleasure in killing,
his aspirations for rulership are thwarted
within the kingdom.

The happy occasions favor the left.
The sad occasions favor the right.
The soldier stands on the left,
while the general stands on the right.
The battle is likened to a funeral.
When many people are killed,
tears and great sorrow are appropriate.
In winning the war,
the victory is celebrated like a funeral.

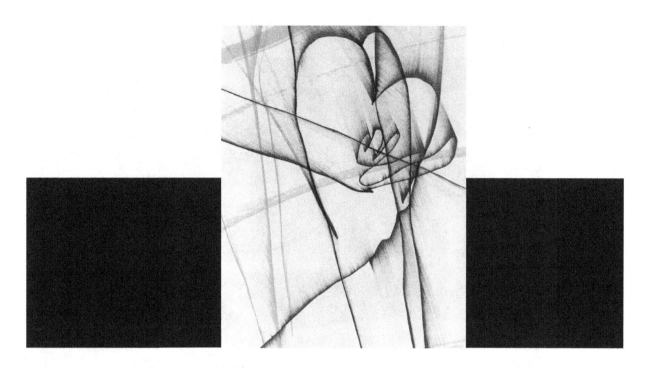

31

Armies are implements of terror and tragedy.
Over the whole earth the masses loathe them.
One who walks the way does not condone their use
except in the most extreme case.
A noble person keeps to the left during peaceful times
and marches to the right during a war.
Since armies are implements of terror and tragedy,
a noble person does not condone them
or become a part of one unless there is no choice.
If he is a part of the victorious force,
he takes no pleasure therein
because anyone who takes pleasure in killing others
is a failure in life.
During favorable times, he promotes the peace.
During unfavorable times, he reluctantly prepares for war.
Standing to the left, the soldier takes the way
of following orders and duty.
Standing to the right, the general takes the way
of leadership and unity.
When the general stands on the right,
it signifies that a life is a precious thing
and when many lives are lost,
one should not take this lightly.
Being a part of the victorious army,
the living should morn the dead.

Thirty-Two

The Tao goes eternally nameless
and although the uncut form is small,
no one can defiantly claim its loyalty.
If rulers and princes were able to hold to it,
the multitudes would give their consent willingly.
Heaven and earth would be joined
and a sweet rain descend.
The people would become fair-minded
without the need for laws and decrees.
Only when it is pulled apart and separated
can there be names.
When names come into existence, it's time to stop.
Knowing the right time to stop keeps you out of trouble.
To the world the Tao is like the ocean and rivers
are to tributaries and streams.

32

The way remains ever undefined.
Though the formless does not take up much space,
no one can employ it for their own use.
If the world's leaders could grab on to it,
all people and nations would bend to their will freely.
Entity and soul would join together.
Peace would prevail.
The people would become of one mind.
There would be no reason for rules and regulations.

When the space is divided, the forms are defined.
When this occurs,
it is important to know when to stop.
It is this stopping that keeps one whole.

In comparing the world to the Tao,
it is like countless rivers and streams
flowing into the sea.

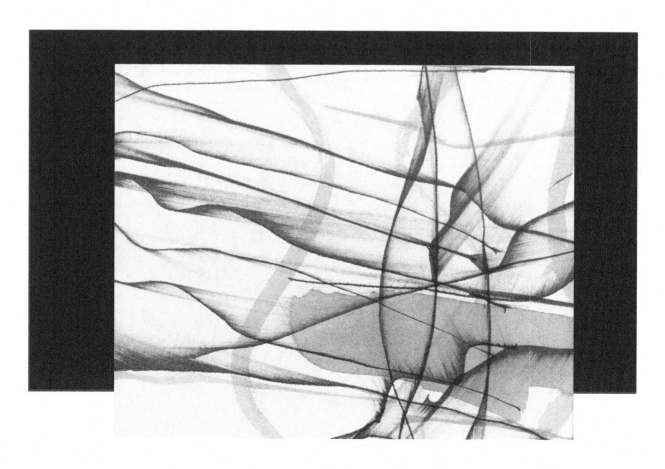

Thirty-Three

One who knows others is clever.
One who knows himself has understanding.
One who controls others has power.
One who controls himself is strong.
One who is satisfied is rich.
One who diligently perseveres reaches the goal.
One who does not lose himself endures.
One who dies but continues has long life.

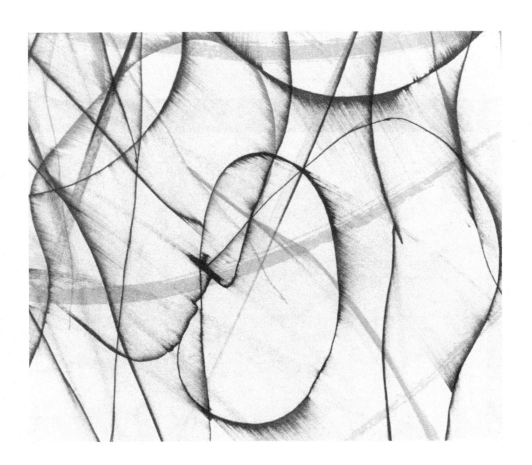

33

Knowing others is intelligence.
Knowing oneself is insight.
Prevailing over others requires an enthusiastic force.
Prevailing over oneself requires discipline.
Being self-sustaining brings wealth.
Being persistent brings endurance.
Don't stray too far from your home.
Don't die and live.

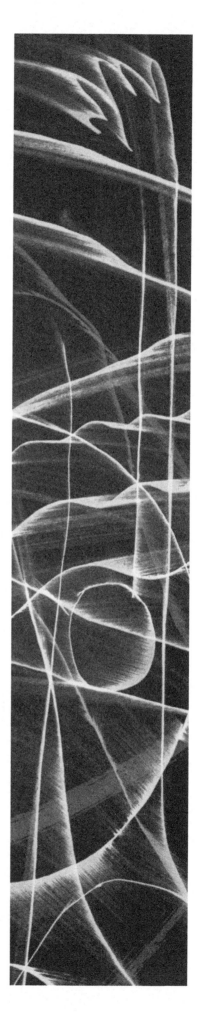

Thirty-Four

The great Tao flows everywhere extending left and right.
The ten thousand beings rely on it for life,
and it doesn't refuse them.
It does the job without taking possession.
It clothes and feeds the ten thousand
without claiming ownership.
Because it goes without desires, it can be called small.
Because the ten thousand beings travel back to it
and it doesn't attempt to control,
it can be called great.
It is because it never claims greatness
that its radiant beauty (greatness) is achieved.

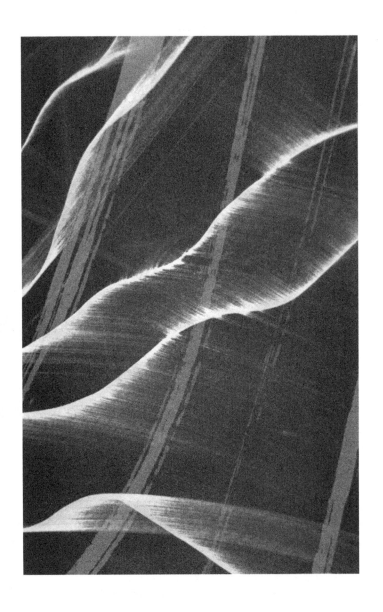

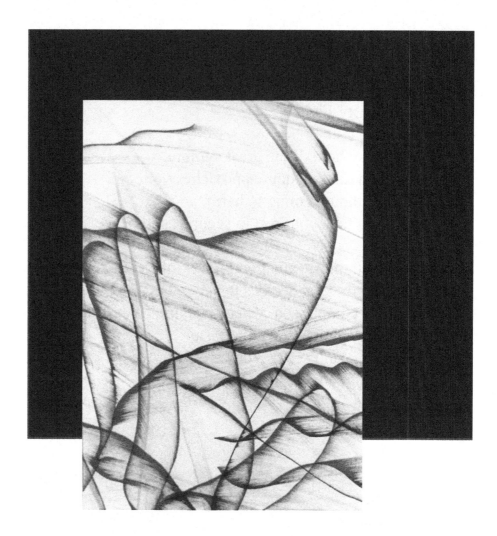

34

The boundless way touches life.
Moving through the darkness, it becomes clarified.
The living count on it for their subsistence,
and it does not exclude anyone.
When things are completed, it does not try to take control.
It protects and provides for the living,
but it doesn't attempt to occupy.
Since it has no drives, it does not take up much space.
Since it doesn't wield authority, it is called boundless.

It is through not recognizing itself as being boundless
that it achieves the state of being boundless.

Thirty-Five

Take hold of the great symbol,
and the kingdom approaches you.
Without coming to harm,
you take your rest in security and peace.

With music and good flavorful food to eat,
the traveler decides to stay.
By comparison, when speaking of the way,
it is mild and without taste.
You can't see it. You can't hear it,
but you will never exhaust it.

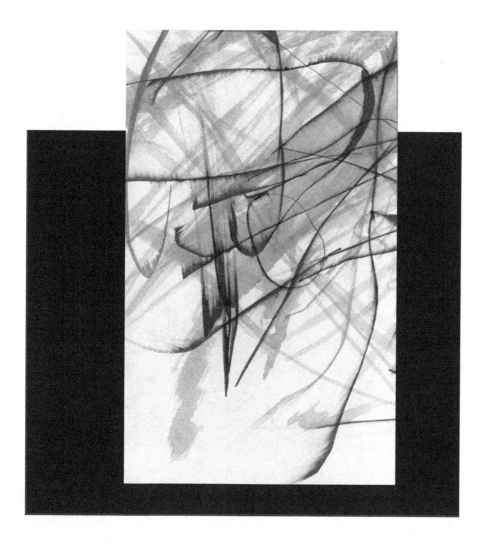

35

Keep a tight grip on the glorious manifestation,
and the world lies open to you.
You are safe from any peril
and can relax in the serene and tranquil.

With dazzling lights, loud rhythmic music,
and wonderful things to look at,
a wanderer settles in.
In contrast, in talking of the Tao,
it is exquisite but does not attract.
You can't see it, and you can't hear it.

Yet, approach it and you will never be dissatisfied.

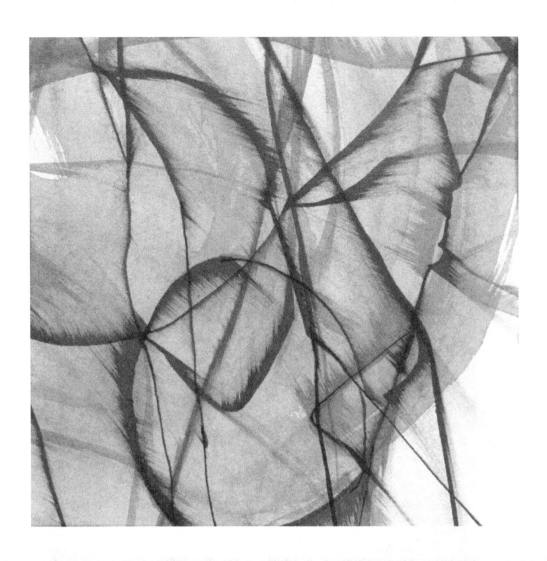

Thirty-Six

What has been shrunk must first have been stretched.
What has been weakened must first have been strong.
What has been brought down must first have been exalted.
What has been taken must first have been given.
This is called the subtle knowledge.
Thus, the gentle and weak overcome the strong and hard.

Fish should not leave the deep water,
and a state's potent weapons should stay out of sight.

36

Make it smaller by enlarging it.
Wear it down by making it robust.
Make it fall by raising it up.

Acquire it by giving it up.

This is called defining the unknown.
Those who bend
when confronted by an intractable impasse will prevail.
Do not venture far from what sustains you.
Have weapons for defense but do not fight.

Thirty-Seven

The Tao never moves but everything gets accomplished.
If rulers and princes were able to hold to it,
the ten thousand beings would grow naturally
of their own accord.
If they still experience desire,
they can return to the uncut form.
There they will find freedom from desire and contention,
a stillness is realized,
and the kingdom is at peace of its own accord.

37

The way does not have a schedule.
Yet with it, nothing goes undone.
If world leaders could utilize it,
the people of earth would inherently progress.
If they should still have drives,
they could go back to the formless.
They would find a refuge from their hungers.
They would achieve a quiet peace.

The world would be a place of tranquility.

Thirty-Eight

A truly pure human being isn't aware of the purity
and thus achieves purity.
The person who lacks purity tries to be pure
and thus lacks purity.
A truly pure human being doesn't move,
has no hidden motives and everything gets accomplished.
The person who lacks purity acts with hidden motives
and many things are not accomplished.
A truly kind person acts without hidden motives.
The moralistic person acts with hidden motives.
When the moralist acts and gets no response,
he rolls up his sleeves in preparation to force the issue.
Therefore, when Tao is lost there is kindness.
When kindness is lost, there is morality and ritual.
Now ritual is the sign of a loss of faith and loyalty
and the beginning of confusion.
Knowing what is to come is a flowering in the way
but the source of foolishness.
Therefore, a truly noble human being
abides in prosperity and not poverty,
partakes of the fruit and not the flowers,
chooses the one and discards the other.

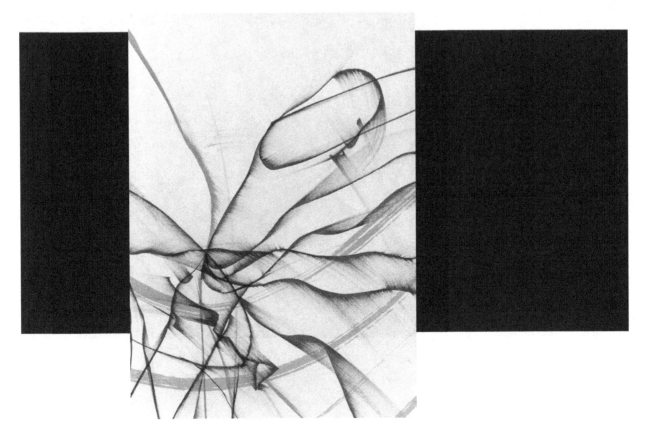

Knowing how to live,
one is not preoccupied with the hows and whys of it.
Not knowing how to live,
one always questions and looks to the hows and whys of it.
Knowing how to live,
one sends commands through the stillness
and, without thought of self-profit, succeeds.
Not knowing how to live,
one always tries for self-gain and self-profit and fails.
Knowing how to live,
one does not think about self-gain or self-loss.
Not knowing how to live,
one is always caught between gain or loss,
between good or bad.
When the way is lost there is virtue.
When virtue is lost, there are good deeds.
When good deeds are lost,
proper behavior and fear of authority are taught.
From here all conviction is lost.
This is the start of chaos.

Intelligence and memory
may be the bright jewel of Tao,
but it is the root of self-deception.
Thus, the spiritual person chooses that
which nourishes
and throws out that which does not.

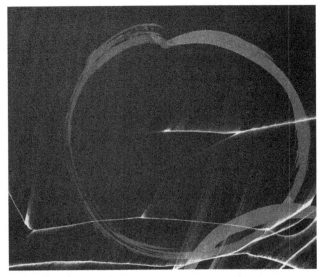

<u>Thirty-Nine</u>

In the distant past, there were those who
came into possession of the oneness.
Through the oneness heaven became pure.
Through the oneness earth became constant.
Through the oneness the gods became powerful.
Through the oneness the valleys became full.
Through the oneness all things became alive.
Through the oneness emperors and dukes
became influential lords of the realm.
All this is because of the oneness.
When purity is lacking heaven shivers.
When constancy is lacking earth shakes.
When power is lacking the gods exhaust themselves.
When fullness is lacking the valleys become deserts.
When the life force is lacking all things return to dust.
When influence is lacking emperors and dukes fall.

Therefore, the great man holds to the common man
as the source.
This is the reason why emperors and dukes call themselves
the lonely, the orphaned and the unfortunate.
Therefore, the great man needs the help
of the common man.
A carriage becomes a carriage by virtue
of many small parts.

Don't tingle like small jade pieces.
Boom like stones (and be whole).

39

Long ago these came into their own
by utilization of the one.
By utilization of the one, the spirit became clarified.
By utilization of the one, the body became stable.
By utilization of the one, God became a virile force.
By utilization of the one, the womb became productive.
By utilization of the one, life became unified.
By utilization of the one, rulers became capable.

These were all by virtue of the one.

Without clarity, the spirit is fragmented.
Without stability, the body quivers.
Without virility, God would exhaust himself.
Without productivity, the womb would wither.
Without unity, life goes unfulfilled.
Without capability, rulers would fail.

Thus, what is mighty has its power
in what is lowly.
The foundation of the high is the low.
This is why great leaders feel
so forlorn, so cut off, so unworthy.
Therefore, a great leader utilizes the services
of each member of society—
For this world becomes unified
from the utilization of its member-parts.
Don't make little snorts.
Be willing to make loud blasts.

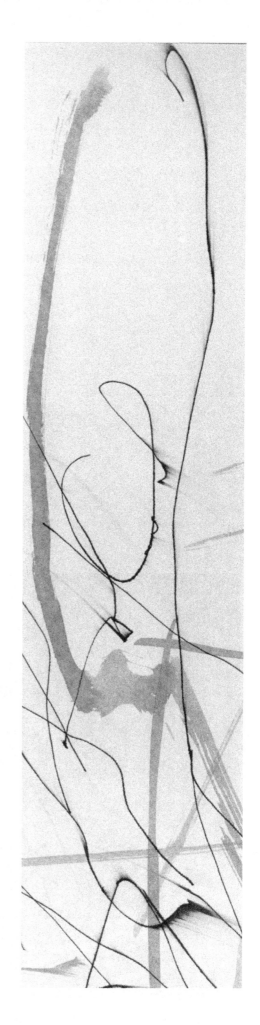

<u>Forty</u>

To return is the inclination of the Tao.
Weakness is the way of the Tao.
The things of this world come from being.
Being comes from not-being.

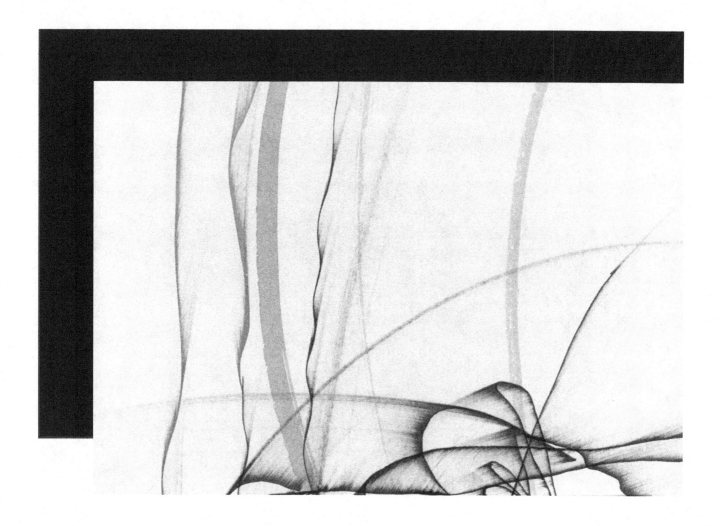

40

Turning back upon itself is the direction of the way.
Flexibility is the path moving through the way.
All living things have definition.
Definition comes from the undefined.

Forty-One

The best student, when hearing of the Tao,
labors to conform to it.
The average student, when hearing of the Tao,
seems to have it one moment and lose it the next.
The inferior student, when hearing of the Tao,
breaks up laughing.
If there is no laughter at it, the Tao is not the true Tao.

There is an old saying that goes like this.
The way of clarity seems dim.
The way that advances forward seems to retreat.
The way of smoothness seems rough.
The highest character seems like a deep valley.
The purist whiteness seems to darken.
The finest character seems at fault.
The strongest character seems listless.
The truest purity seems tarnished.
The complete square has no corners.
The complete bowl takes a long time in production.
The complete sound goes almost unheard.
The complete form is without shape.

The Tao hides itself in namelessness.
Yet, it is the Tao that excels at helping the living
and bringing life to completion.

41

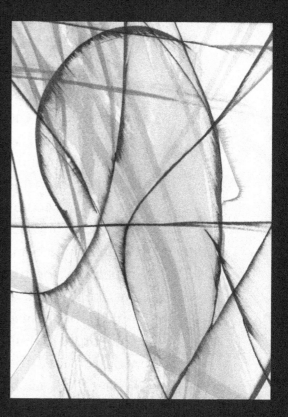

When the receptive student hears of the way,
he strives to become a part of it.
When the common man hears of the way,
he holds to it for a moment and lets go in the next.
When an ignorant man hears of the way,
he begins to laugh aloud at it.
If there is no laughter accompanying it,
the way would not be the way.

An old proverb says this.
My path to enlightenment appears unclear.
My path to improvements appears to regress.
My path to balance appears like a bumpy road.
My path to goodness appears like a faint light
shining in a barren womb.
The innocent way is corrupt.
The righteous way is twisted.
The fervent way is worn out.
The clearest way is through the darkness.

The body seems to be self sufficient.
The construction of ones true home
seems to take a long time in the making.
The truth seems difficult to discern.
The spiritual body seems without an outline.

Tao is hidden in its lack of definition.
Even so, it is the Tao
which sustains the living and brings a wholeness
and a completeness to our lives.

Forty-Two

The Tao conceives of the one.
One conceives two.
Two conceives three.
The three conceive the ten thousand beings.
The ten thousand beings have the darkness
at their backs while facing the light.
Harmony is achieved from a blending and a unifying
of these two forces.
All men hate being lonely, being orphaned
or being unfortunate.
Yet, emperors and dukes use these words
to describe themselves.
Sometimes a thing gains from its being decreased
and decreases from each gain.
What others teach I also teach:
a violent man dies a violent death.

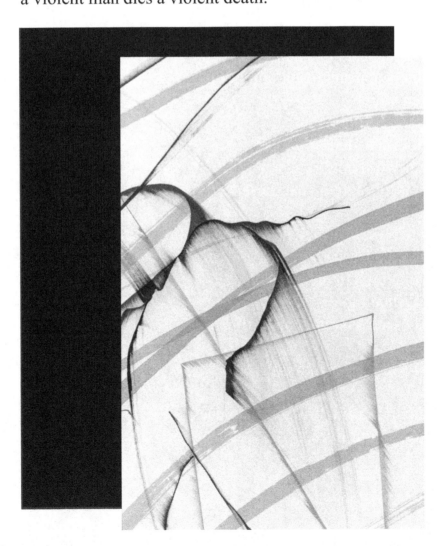

42

The way gives birth to soul.
Soul gives birth to entity.
Soul and entity give birth to desire.
The three give birth to the living.
The living are pushed from behind
by the darkness (yin energy)
as they attempt to hold to the light (yang energy).
A balance comes from the mixing
of these two powers.
People can't stand being forlorn,
cut off and unworthy.
Yet, great leaders speak of themselves
in these terms.
Some things profit from becoming smaller
and decline when made large.
I teach the same thing that others teach:
a cruel and heartless person
dies a cruel and heartless death.
This is the foundation of my instruction.

Forty-Three

The softest thing in the world
wears down the hardest.
That which has no substance
enters that which has no space.
From this I know the merit of taking no action.

Teaching without words
and the merit of taking no action,
these are things only a very few of us
in this world attain.

43

The gentle overcomes the rigid.
The spirit can penetrate
every crevice of the universe.
From this I know the importance of not moving
in order to get things done.
From this I know
that teaching can go on without speaking words.
From this I know
the importance of not struggling.
From this I know
there are only a very few of us
are able to utilize these words.

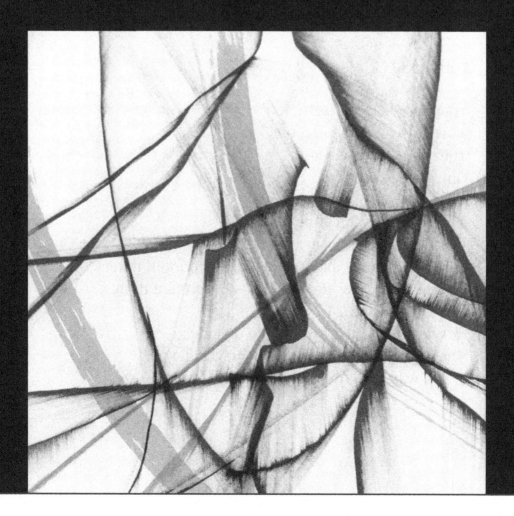

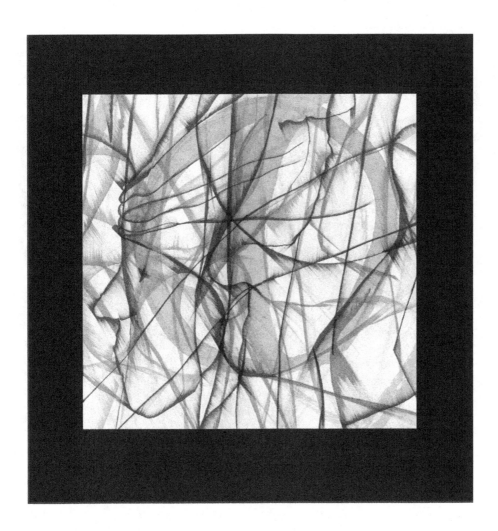

Forty-Four

Your name or your self,
which do you cherish more?
Your self or your things,
which is worth more?
Your loss or your gain,
which is more defeating?
Therefore, he who has a yearning for things
overspends and exhausts the more important things.
He who stockpiles loses the most important things.

Be content and you will not be disgraced.
Know when to stop and you avert danger.
In this way, you live and endure.

44

Body or soul,
which one do you value more?
Your soul or your individuality,
which one do you prize more?

Poverty or wealth,
which one brings the greatest loss?

Thus, those who follow the body
to the exclusion of their souls
deprive themselves of the essence of life.
Continue building up and following the body's drives
and eventually you lose your life.

Be satisfied with yourself and what you have,
and you will not lose yourself.
Stopping before you've committed yourself
keeps you out of harm.

Go with the Tao, and you find life and permanence.

Forty-Five

Great achievement appears unfinished;
yet, use will never weaken it.
Great fullness appears empty;
yet, use will never exhaust it.
Great straightness appears bent.
Great skill appears awkward.
Great eloquence appears tight lipped.
Movement overcomes the cold.
Stillness overcomes the heat.
Purity and stillness:
with these, you can rule the kingdom.

45

The ultimate perfection seems to have flaws;
that is why no one is afraid to use it.
The greatest wealth seems worthless;
that is why it is abused so much.
The highest truth seems a delusion.
The finest talent seems inept.
The most articulate seems uncommunicative.

Enlightenment triumphs over a lack of unity.
Contentment triumphs over all hungers.
Goodness and contentment:
these bring to completion everything in this world.

Forty-Six

When the way gains the ascendancy in the kingdom,
the swiftest horses are used for hauling manure.
When the way loses influence over the kingdom,
war horses are bred at the outskirts of the city.

There is no greater fault
than hanging on to too many desires.
There is no greater calamity than a lack of contentment.
There is no greater misery than wanting
what you cannot have.
Therefore, be content
and you will always have enough.

46

When Tao is unmistakably in the world,
the people put their energy into the feeding
and clothing of humanity.
When Tao is not easily perceived in the world,
the people put their energy
into enormous engines of destruction.

There isn't anything worse
than continually hungering after things.
There isn't anything more troublesome
than not accepting things as they are.
There isn't any sorrow more persistent
than coveting what others have.

Thus, being satisfied with what you have,
you are able to attain an enduring abundance.

Forty-Seven

Without opening your door and stepping outside,
you can know the totality of the world.
Without looking through your window,
you can see heaven's way.
The further out you go, the less you know.
Therefore, a wise person knows
without roaming about
and completes everything without doing.

47

From your own home,
and without taking a step outside,
you can know the myriad paths traveling
through the world.
From your own home, looking out the window,
you can come into contact with the spirit.

As your understanding and insight increase,
your accumulation of knowledge decreases.

Thus, a spiritual person achieves without traveling,
sees without looking
and traverses but does not move.

Forty-Eight

In the quest for learning, each day something is acquired.
In the quest for the Tao, each day something is lost.
In the constant loss, less and less is done
until pursuing ceases.
When you stop pursuing, everything gets done.

The kingdom is won by leaving things alone.
In tampering with the kingdom,
you never attain the realm.

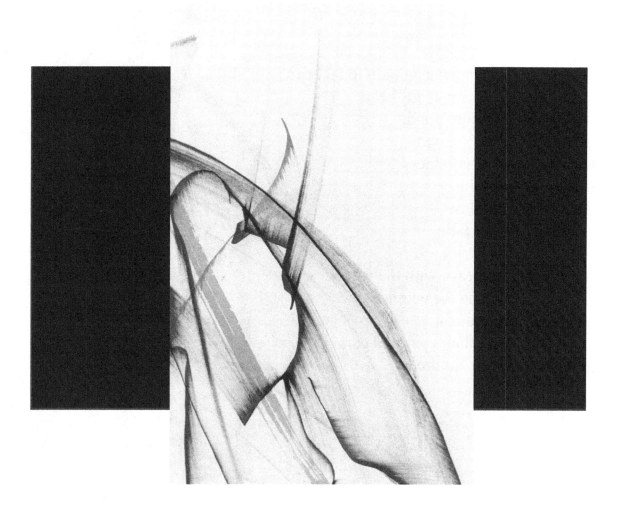

48

When acquiring a body of knowledge,
you need to get the facts one at a time.
When acquiring the Tao,
you get rid of the facts in order to behold.

When striving comes to a standstill
and all movement stops,
you gain everything from the loss.

In conquering the world,
you are successful when you give up
always trying to fix things.
In trying to fix things, you lose yourself.

Forty-Nine

The wise person doesn't have an individual heart.
He takes the people's heart as his heart.
I am good to those that are good.
I am good to those that are bad—
For this is the virtue of goodness.
I have faith in the faithful.
I have faith in the faithless—
For this is the virtue of faith.

The wise person is at peace with the world.
Yet, his existence among the people
causes them great confusion.
All the people overtax their eyes and ears.
He treats them just like children.

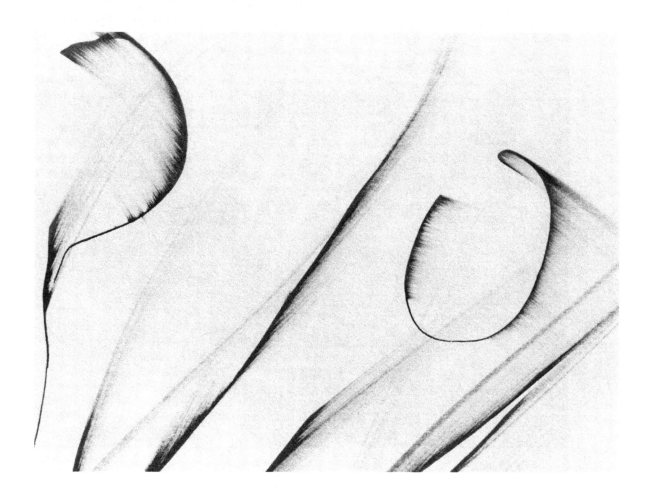

49

The spiritual person doesn't have a belief of his own
but accepts as his own the people's beliefs.
I treat well the good beliefs,
and I forgive the bad ones.
Through this, I gain a wealth of goodness.
I empathize with the religious.
I empathize with the non-religious.
Through this, I gain a wealth of belief.

The spiritual person is joined to the world.
He unites his mind with those of others.
The ordinary man strains his eyes and ears
just to perceive him.
He treats them all as if they were his own children.

Fifty

Man's path moves from life to death.
From ten, there are three who move toward life.
From ten, there are three who move toward death.
From ten, there are three who value life
but move toward death.
Why is this so?
Because of their possessiveness in life.

There is a saying.
He who knows how to live can roam the land
without meeting tiger or rhinoceros.
He marches into battle
and avoids being touched by sharp weapons.
The rhinoceros finds no space for horn to gore.
The tiger finds no space for claws to sink.
The sharp weapon finds no space to penetrate.
Why is it so?
Because there is no space for death to enter.

50

If moving from inside to outside,
if going in or out brings life or death,
if being open and receptive brings life
and by being closed and unyielding
one reaches the point of death,
then there are thirteen companions,
the four limbs and nine outside organs
and openings which bring life.
Then there are thirteen companions,
the four limbs and nine outside organs
and openings which bring death.
There are also thirteen companions
who live but travel to their death.
How can this be?
Because they multiply their desires.

It is said
that he who is careful and protective
of the life given to him
can wander over the whole world
without being endangered by man or wild beast.
He goes into battle and is not touched by bullet or bomb.
Neither man nor wild beast can find a place to strike.
The bullet and bomb find no place to enter.
How can this be?

Because there is no place for death to touch.

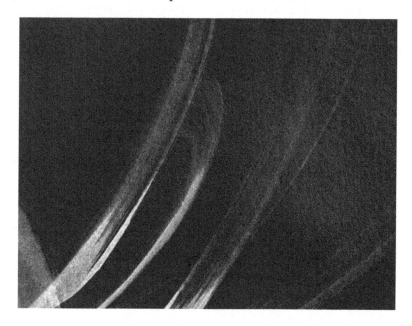

Fifty-One

Tao conceives all life.
Its goodness nourishes them.
The things of the world give them form.
Their environment is a strong influence.
Therefore, the ten thousand beings honor Tao
and glorify its goodness.
Honoring the way is not commanded
but chosen freely.
Therefore, the way conceives all life
and its goodness nourishes them,
helps them grow and develop.
It shelters them, feeds them, nurses and protects them.
It conceives all life yet renounces any possession.
It helps the living but never asks for thanks.
It guides but does not control.
This is called the mysterious virtue.

51

Tao gives life to all things.
Its nature sustains them.
Matter gives them a form.
The influences shape them.
Knowingly and unknowingly,
every living thing adores the Tao,
and gives thanks to its nature.
This adoration is given voluntarily
and is not ordained.
Thus, the Tao gives life to all things
and its nature sustains them
and encourages them to expand and evolve.
It houses, nurtures and is a sanctuary for them.
It gives life to all things
but relinquishes ownership.
It encourages and sustains the living
but doesn't ask for gratitude.
It instructs but does not attempt to control.
This is the hidden nature.

Fifty-Two

The world had its beginning
which can be called mother of the world.
When you know the mother,
you can also know the sons.
When you know the sons,
return to holding to the mother
and to the end of your days you will not be endangered.
Keep your mouth shut.
Shut your doors
and you will never tire.
Unplug the passageways,
begin to move about
and to the end of your days you will not find fulfillment.
See what is small and attain clear sight.
Yield and know strength.
Use the light to comprehend
and you will not be harmed.
This is known as following the established fact.

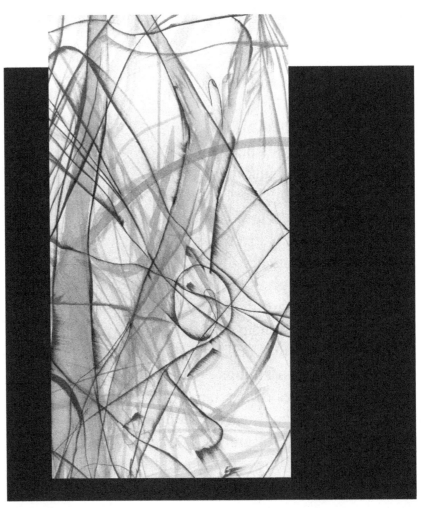

52

There is a beginning to the world.
She is regarded as the mother of the world.
Perceiving the mother,
you can also gain knowledge of her manifestations.
When you have gained knowledge of her manifestations,
go back to her and you will never be in danger
throughout your life.

Stop excessive talk.
Conserve your energy
and avoid exhaustion.
Be talkative.
Waste your energy
by going in five directions at once,
and you will never be able to get things straightened out.
Become aware of what cannot be clearly perceived
and achieve enlightenment.
With this you are protected,
with this you are following the tried and true.

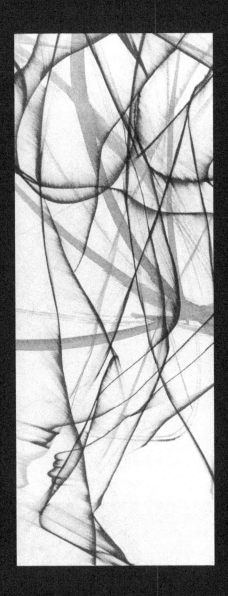

Fifty-Three

If I have just a little insight,
I would walk the path through the great way
and fear only the detours.
The great way is simple and easy.
Yet, people love to get sidetracked.
While the court is kept sparkling clean,
the fields are full of weeds
and granaries are empty.

So they dress up in their finest clothes
with their sharp swords by their sides.
They overdose on food and drink.
They have an excess of wealth.
This is called an invitation for plundering.
This is to detour from the way.

53

If I use but a small amount of sensibility,
I will walk the road of the vast Tao
and will only fear straying from it.
The vast way is straight and easy to travel,
but people enjoy their excursions.

While nations spend their surpluses
on armaments and foolishness,
most of the world goes hungry.

Then there are those among us
who have more than they can ever hope to use.
They spend their lives overloading and overindulging.
This is called robbing the life out of the poor.
This is to stray from the way.

Fifty-Four

What is firmly rooted will not be plucked up.
What is firmly embraced will not slip loose.
This sacrifice from our posterity is an endless process.
Develop it in yourself
and your goodness will be real.
Develop it in the family
and the family's goodness abounds.
Develop it in the village
and the village's goodness lasts.
Develop it in the state
and the state's goodness becomes all-inclusive.
Develop it throughout the kingdom
and the kingdom's goodness becomes universal.
Therefore, by comparing yourself with others,
you are able to assess others.
By comparing the family with others,
you are able to assess the family.
By comparing the state with others,
you are able to assess the state.
By comparing the kingdom with others,
you are able to assess the kingdom.
How do I know life is like this?
By this.

54

What is well-founded will not easily
be pulled apart.
What is held securely will not slip loose.
Your children and your children's children
will carry your memory with them.

Make this way manifest in your life.

Make this manifest in yourself,
and your character is genuine.
Make this manifest in your family,
and the character of the family is whole.
Make this manifest in the community,
and the character of the community endures.
Make this manifest in the nation,
and the character of the nation is bountiful.
Make this manifest in the world,
and the character of the world is pure.
Therefore,
look at yourself
before you attempt to look at others.
Look at your family
before you attempt to look at other families.
Look at your community
before you attempt to look at other communities.
Look at your nation
before you attempt to look at other nations.
Look at your world
before you attempt to look at other worlds.

Fifty-Five

The person who has abundant goodness
is like an infant.
Poisonous insects will not sting it.
Fierce animals will not pounce on it.
Birds of prey will not plunge down on it.
Although bones are soft and muscles weak,
his grip is strong.
Although he has not experienced the joining together
of male and female, his manhood stirs.
This is the culmination of essence.
Although he shouts all day, he does not become hoarse.
This is the culmination of harmony.

To know harmony is to find the constant.
To know the constant is enlightening.
But to be inflexible about living life to the fullest extent,
this results in grief.

When the mind tries to dominate the living essence,
this is losing one's way.

Since things that reach their prime begin to age,
what goes counter to the way meets an early end.

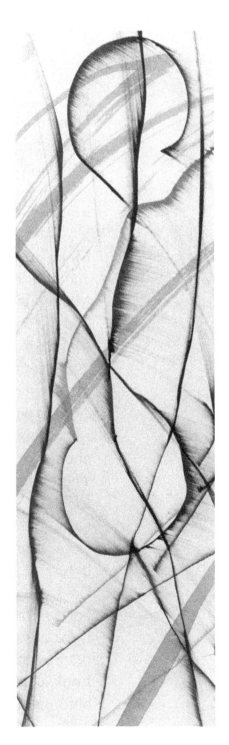

55

One who has an ample amount of virtue
is childlike.
Not bothered by the tiny gnawing things in life,
not harmed through violence,
not attacked from the unknown,
one is protected.

The physique may not be heavily muscled,
but he enjoys robust health.
Although he doesn't look different from other humans,
it is his sincerity and his dedication
in keeping to a cheerful attitude about life
which sets him apart.
This brings vitality.
He works throughout the day,
yet it does not exhaust him.
This points to a complete balance of energy.
To achieve a complete balance of energy
is to come face to face with the everlasting.
To come face to face with the everlasting is to be illumined.

But to attempt to manipulate and control the life force
brings on the aging process.
To go beyond what is natural
in building up strength or sexual prowess,
this is disastrous.

Fifty-Six

He that knows does not speak.
He that speaks does not know.
Keep your mouth shut.
Shut your doors.
Make smooth the sharpness.
Untie the knots.
Decrease the glare.
Travel the tried and true and merge with the dust.
This is the mysterious uniformity.

He who attains this
cannot be kept in or held back,
cannot be made an advantage or a loss,
cannot be honored or disgraced.
Therefore, he is always honored in the kingdom.

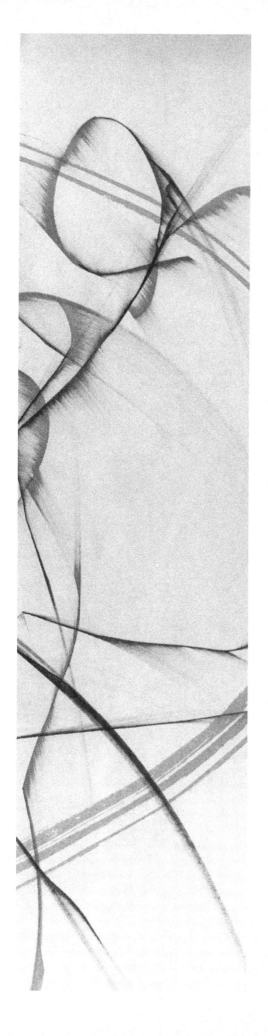

56

He that apprehends knows
he cannot impart an experience
by speaking about it.
He that doesn't apprehend always tries to explain
what cannot be explained.

Stop excessive talk.
Bend your unyieldingness.
End your confusion.
Dim your brightness.
Continually use the path
that has brought you your success.

This brings an awesome balance.

He that reaches this transcends the duality
of the world.
He can't be influenced or moved.
He can't be made either an asset or a liability.
He can't be touched by praise or blame.
Thus, he is praised throughout the world.

Fifty-Seven

Be trustworthy when governing the kingdom.
Be crafty when going to war.
Win the kingdom by not intervening.
How do I know—because of this.
The more thou shalt nots in the kingdom,
the more impoverished the people.
The more finely honed people's tools,
the more confusion in the kingdom.
The more artful and ingenious the people,
the more cunning the technology.
The more laws and regulations given,
the more thieves and robbers.

Therefore, the wise person says:
I do nothing,
and the people are transformed.
I love calmness,
and the people are self-correcting.
I do not intervene,
and the people are prosperous.
I am without desires,
and the people are as unsophisticated
as the uncarved form.

57

In governing be direct.
In waging war be devious.
In conquering the world, leave things alone.
How is this so—from this.
Adding prohibitions means
a decrease in personal freedoms.
Producing large numbers of weaponry
brings nothing but chaos to the world.
Promoting ingenuity and manipulation
is the foundation for the most erratic science.
Multiplying the edicts and ordinances
brings an increase in crime and thievery.

Thus, the spiritual person says,
if I act by not moving,
the people will decide to make the necessary changes.
If I love the stillness,
the people will enjoy the freedom and reform themselves.
If I am not an employer,
the people gain the incentive and become rich.
If I have no desires,
the people are truthful and straightforward.

Fifty-Eight

When the government is quiet and undemanding,
the people are simple and prosperous.
When the government is in motion,
the people are crafty and dissatisfied.
It is upon misery that happiness sits.
It is beneath happiness that misery crouches.
Who knows what the future has in store?
It is when the government attempts to straighten
what is crooked
that even the good becomes warped.
People have been confused for a long time.

Therefore, the wise person has integrity
and does not cut others down,
performs his duties without harming others,
is lustrous but not bedazzling.

When a ruler is calm and friendly,
the people are forthright and open.
When a ruler is cold and calculating,
the people will be two-faced and deceitful.

The origin of happiness lies in misery.
Misery lurks behind happiness.

Who can know what a great ruler is like?

Either the ruler stops bothering the people
or the people become grotesque abnormalities.
What was once good turns into something evil.
Mankind's ignorance lasts for a long time.

Therefore, the spiritual person is truthful and honest
but is not cutting.
He is responsible without injuring others.
He is honorable but does not punish others.
His light shines but is not glaring.

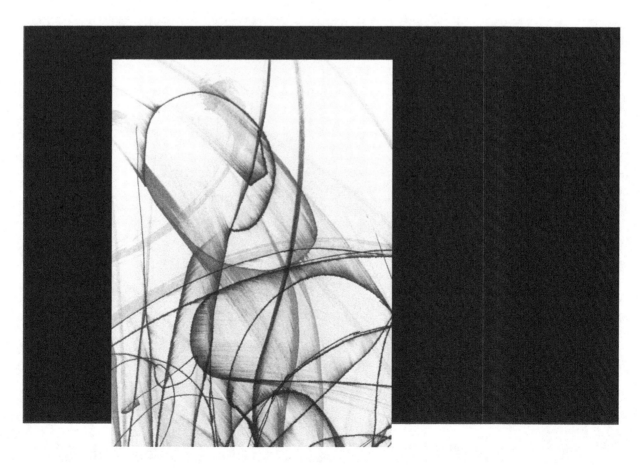

Fifty-Nine

In ruling the people and serving heaven,
there is nothing like having an amiable nature.
Because he has an amiable nature,
he is able to follow the path from its inception.
Walking the way from its inception
means he has built up an abundant amount of goodness.
With an abundant amount of goodness
there is nothing that he cannot overcome,
and there is no limit to his overcoming.
Since there isn't anyone who knows his limit,
he is beyond limitation
and is fit to rule the kingdom.

Because he follows the mother, he will long endure.
This is called the path of roots going deeply
into the firm ground—the way to longevity
and a limitless vision.

59

In the governing of men
and in the service of the spirit,
there isn't anything better than a moderate
non-violent person.
Through this, from the very beginning,
he is able to bring himself into accord with the Tao.
Bringing himself into accord with the Tao,
it can be said that he has built up
a wealth of virtue.
Virtue that cannot be beaten down
has no limitations.
Because there is no one who knows his boundaries,
he has no limitations.
The whole world lies open to him.

Since he holds to the mother and possesses the world,
he attains longevity.
This is known as building a strong foundation.
This is the road to eternal life and boundless insight.

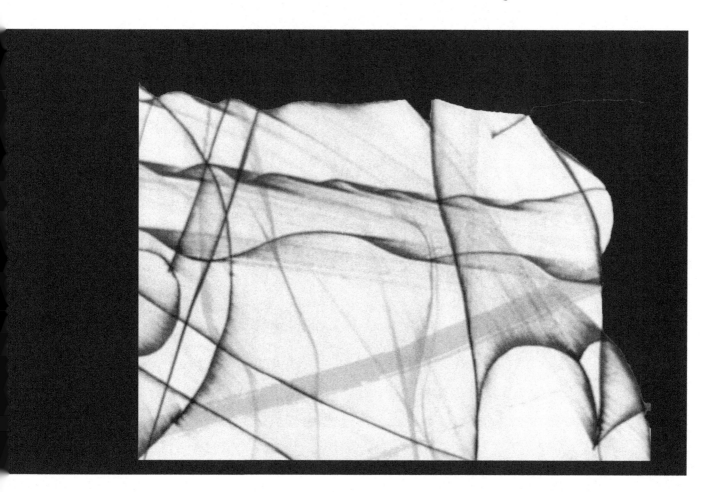

Sixty

Governing a large state is like cooking small fish.
If the kingdom is governed in harmony
with the Tao,
not even the spirit world has its power.
This is not to say
that the spirits have lost their powers.
On the contrary, they still have their powers.
Yet, they do no harm to the people.
A wise person also does no harm to the people.
Since no harm has been done,
that goodness belongs to us all.

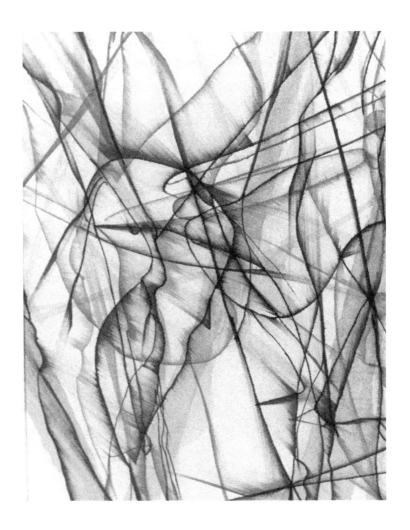

60

Ruling a large nation
resembles the frying of a small fish.
When the nation is ruled in agreement
with the way,
even daemonic forces lose their influences.
This isn't to say that daemonic forces
have no influence.
Rather, what it means is
that they will not impair anyone.
The spiritual person, too, does not impair anyone.
If through the utilization of these two powers
no impairment is incurred by anyone,
then the virtue gained is shared by everyone.

Sixty-One

Like a river flowing downstream,
a large state should be the world's meeting place
where divergent forces unite.
This is like the female of the world.
The female always overcomes the male
by keeping still.
In keeping still, she takes the lower place.
Thus a large state, in taking the lower place,
overcomes the small state.
The small state, in taking the lower place,
overcomes the large state.
Therefore, the large puts itself below
to gain others
while the small, by virtue of being small,
naturally takes the lower place
to use others.
So the large state needs more people
while the small state needs to be useful.
In order for both to get what they want,
the large should take the lower place.

61

Like mountain streams flowing down to a common source,
a great nation should be humble,
serving as a place for different people,
different thoughts coming together.

All living things under heaven
need a body (small nation).
The body receives its life
through the soul (great nation) by remaining still.
Remaining still, the body rests under the soul.
Therefore, if a great nation remains receptive
to a smaller nation,
then it receives life from the smaller nation.
If a smaller nation remains receptive
to a great nation,
then it receives life from the greater nation.
Thus, everyone profits from taking the lower place,
remaining still, receptive and humble.

Sixty-Two

The way is the origin of the ten thousand beings,
the treasure of the good man
and the caretaker of the bad.
Beautiful words buy high honor.
Beautiful deeds bring a man prominence.

Even the bad man, why should we reject him.

Therefore, when the emperor is crowned
and as the three ducal ministers are appointed,
without moving from your seat, send out your presents
from the way.
This is preferable to presents of jade
and a team of four horses.

Why did the ancients treasure the Tao?
Wasn't it once said
that when you travel the way, you find what you seek,
and you escape the sinful nature that pursues you.
Therefore, the way is the most valued
of the kingdom.

62

Tao is a home to all things.
It's what the good man cherishes.
It's a sanctuary for wrong doers.
Beautiful words can be bought.
Good deeds can be given as a present.
Although there are wrong doers in the world,
why should we abandon them?

Therefore, at the swearing in ceremonies
for high ranking governmental officials,
a gift far more precious than gold
would be an offering of the Tao.

Why did the people of antiquity so love the Tao?
Has it not been said
that you find what you have been looking for,
and you avoid what has tormented and confused you.

Thus, the Tao is the most beloved of the world.

Sixty-Three

Follow the way of taking no action; don't intervene.
Taste the taste of the tasteless.
Broaden what is small; do more with less.
Act with kindness to those who would mistreat you.
Before the difficult task becomes overwhelming,
make your plans.
Great things are achieved in small increments.
The difficult thing must once have originated
in what was easy.
Great things originate in a small thing.
Therefore, the wise person
doesn't attempt anything great and achieves greatness.
He who promises lightly
often finds it difficult to keep his faith.
He who takes things lightly
often meets with many difficulties.
Thus, even a wise person
must take care of difficulties.
It is for this reason he is never overwhelmed by them.

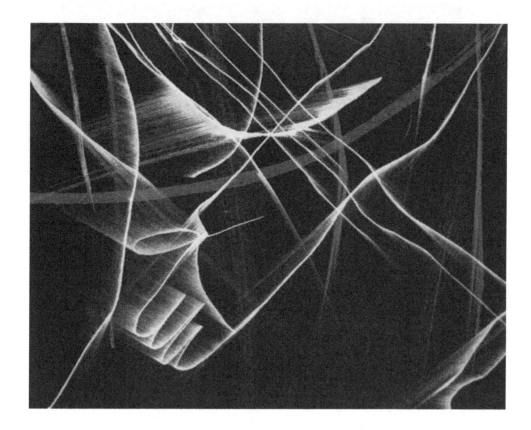

63

Accomplish by not doing.
Labor without tampering with.
Be in touch with the formless.
Enlarge the small; multiply the scarce.

Repay hatred with love.

Have a plan for what is bothersome
before it gets the better of you.
Make something great by beginning with something small.
What is complicated originates in what is simple.
What is great originates in what is small.
Therefore, the spiritual person never thinks about
doing great things,
and that is why he accomplishes great things.

If you make promises, then fulfill them.
Don't take important matters lightly.
Be serious about them, or you're likely to have problems.
Thus, because the spiritual person faces difficulties,
he's never oppressed by them.

Sixty-Four

The peace is easily preserved while things are at rest.
What has not taken shape can be avoided
before it starts.
What is still brittle is easily broken.
What is still minute is easily dispersed.
Deal with a thing before it manifests itself.
Maintain order before confusion prevails.
A tree trunk as large as a man's outstretched arms
grows from a tiny sprout.
A terrace nine stories high starts with a shovel of dirt.
A thousand mile journey starts beneath one foot.

Leave it alone; try to hold on to it and you've lost it.

Because the wise person takes no action, he spoils nothing.
Because he doesn't try to hold on, nothing slips away.
A person's project is always spoiled
when he's on the verge of success.
Be as careful with the end as with the beginning
and nothing will be spoiled.
Therefore, the wise person: rejects desire;
does not value precious things;
learns what cannot be learned;
retrieves what the ten thousand beings have lost
in order to help men find their true natures.
He strives not to intervene.

64

What is latent is easily held.
What hasn't materialized is easily evaded.
The fragile is easily broken.
The tiny is easily scattered.
Take care of things before they happen.
Support the peace before chaos prevails.
A big tree begins with a small seed.
Greatness is attained by building up small things.

Cease tampering; stop your possessiveness.

Therefore, the spiritual person doesn't struggle
and doesn't ruin anything.
He does not snatch at things and thus,
he does not lose his grip.
People's enterprises are often ruined
just when they are about to succeed.
Be as patient with endings as you are with beginnings,
and you won't ruin anything.

Thus, the spiritual person: desires not to desire;
doesn't hunger after things that are hard to obtain;
learns what can't be imparted or taught;
returns what the people have lost
so that they can know the true nature of things.

He works at not tampering.

Sixty-Five

From ancient times,
those rulers who were travelers of the way
did not attempt to enlighten the people
but to keep them unknowing.
The reason why the people are so difficult to govern
is that they are too clever.
Thus, he who rules a state with cleverness
does harm to the state.
Not ruling the state with cleverness
is a blessing to the land.
These are two models.
To know the models is called mysterious goodness.
The mysterious goodness is deep and far-reaching.
It returns things to their source.
It achieves a complete wholeness.

65

In the distant past, the followers of Tao
did not try to impart their knowledge to others
but instead used it to unify the world
and preserve people's innocence.
Why is it so difficult to rule?
Isn't it because people get narrow-minded about things.
Therefore, the leader who governs with artificial knowledge
causes divisions and injures the nation.
The leader who governs with innocence
is a boon to the nation.

These are two examples.
Understanding the hidden significance is a virtue—
For it has the power to return things
to their original state.
It brings back our innocence.

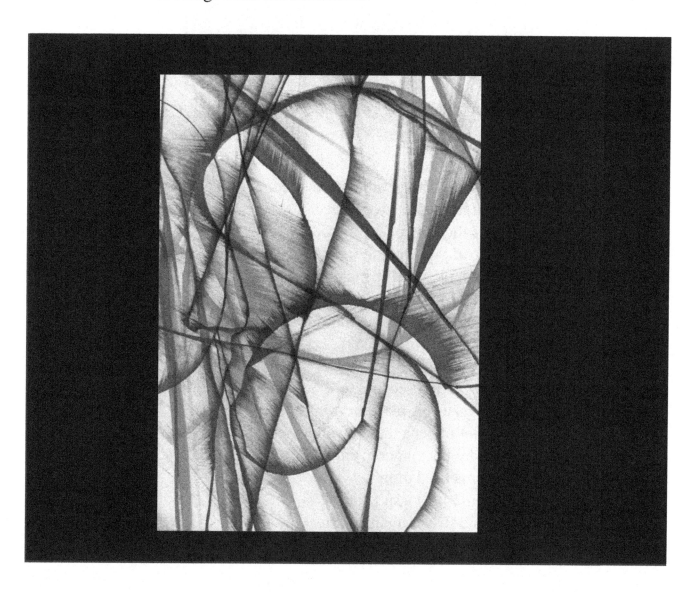

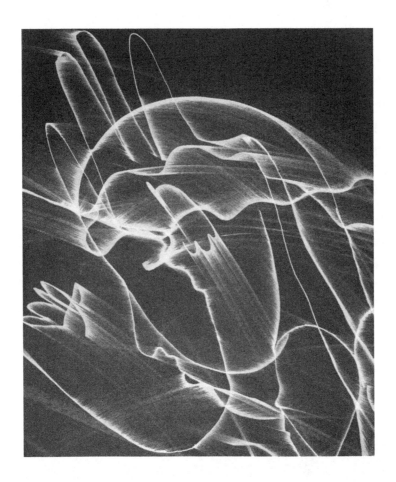

Sixty-Six

The sea is the king of a hundred streams
because it takes the lower place.
Thus, it is the king of a hundred streams.
Therefore, if you want to be over the people,
you must put yourself beneath them.
If you want to lead the people,
you must follow from behind them.
Thus, when the wise person
takes his place over the people,
the people do not see him as a burden.
When he takes his place in front of the people,
he does not impede their advancement.
That is why the kingdom cares for him
and never is tired of him.
It is because he doesn't strive
that no one strives against him.

66

Be unselfish and you will always succeed.
If you wish to lead the people,
you must first renounce yourself.

A leader is also a follower.

Thus, when the spiritual person attains his high position
the people don't view him as an obligation.
In standing before the people,
he does nothing to slow their forward progress.
That is why, knowingly or unknowingly,
the world takes good care of him
and supports him.
Because he threatens no one,
there is no one who wishes to harm him.

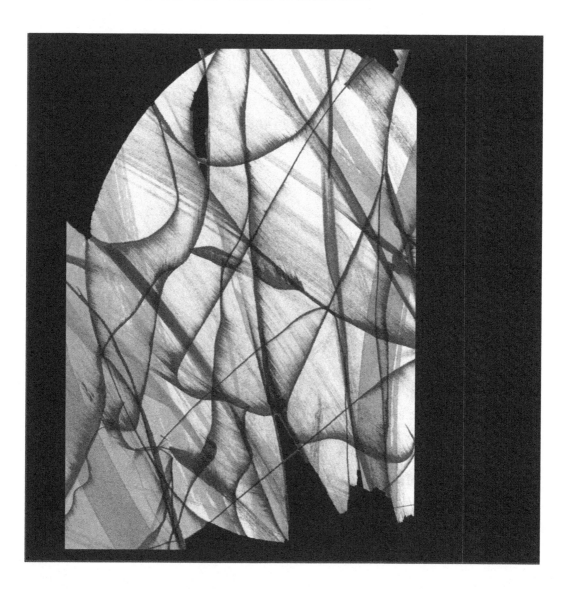

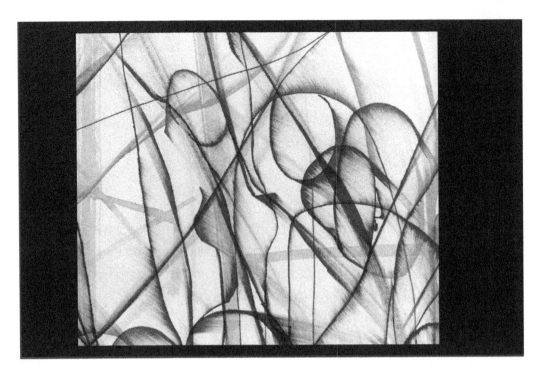

<u>Sixty-Seven</u>

The whole world says that my way is great
and is like nothing else.
It is because it is great that it seems like nothing else.
If it looked like anything else,
long ago it would have become inconsequential.
I have three treasures I keep close to me:
the first is love;
the second is moderation;
the third is daring not to be the front runner
in the kingdom.
With love, I can be without fear.
With moderation, I can be bighearted.
From daring not to be the front runner,
I can be a leader.

If people abandon love and attempt to be without fear,
if people abandon moderation and attempt to be bighearted,
if people abandon daring not to be the front runner
and attempt to be a leader,
this is sure death.
With love, you will win the battle
with an unbeatable defense.
What heaven supports is guarded
with the gift of love.

67

The entire world states that my Tao
is infinite and is beyond compare
but that it lacks definition.
Because it is infinite,
you cannot compare it with anything else.
If you could liken it to something else,
then it would have passed away long ago.
I prize three things above all else:
the first is compassion;
the second is abundance;
the third is striving not to have contention.
Having compassion, I can be valiant.
Having abundance, I can be generous.
Having no contention, I can be a ruler.

If you give up compassion but strive to be valiant,
if you give up abundance but strive to be generous,
if you give up having no contention
but strive to be a ruler,
this is begging for an early end.

Through the use of compassion you will prevail
with an impenetrable defense.
Whatever the spirit sustains is protected
with compassion.

<u>Sixty-Eight</u>

The good soldier doesn't seem warlike.
The good fighter doesn't lose his temper.
The good champion doesn't take revenge.
The good employer doesn't act the superior.
This is known as the virtue of no contention.
This is known as applying the usefulness of others.
This is known as the ladder men climb to reach heaven.

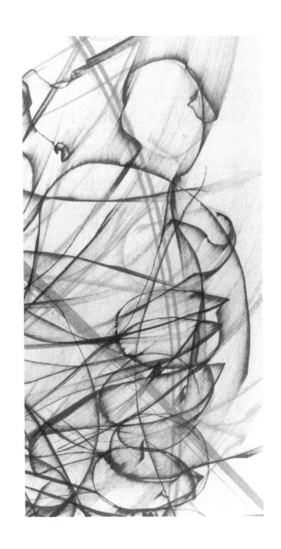

68

The superior warrior does not appear to be deadly.
The superior fighter does not show anger.
The superior victor does not avenge.
The superior employer
does not stand above the people.
Call this the virtue of having no animosity.
Call this understanding how to carry out
the usefulness of others.
Call this the tool men use to get
in touch with their souls.

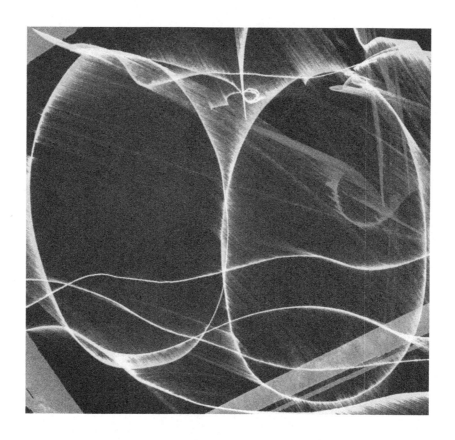

Sixty-Nine

The tacticians have a saying.
Best not to play the host,
better to be the guest.
Best not to advance an inch,
better to step back a foot.
This is known as
marching without using your legs,
rolling up your sleeves without using your arms,
defeating the enemy without using your forces.

There is no greater misfortune than misjudging
the enemy.
By misjudging, you almost lose what you treasure.
Therefore, when two opposing forces meet,
the champion is the one who receives no joy in victory.

69

The soldiers have a saying:
I must not initiate the festivities.
Instead, I will be a part of the welcoming reception.
I must not go forward an inch.
Instead, I will drop back a foot.

This is taking action without antagonizing.

There is nothing worse than underestimating
the enemy.
When you underestimate the enemy,
you can lose what you cherish most.
Thus, when combatants clash,
the winner is not pleased with the state of things.

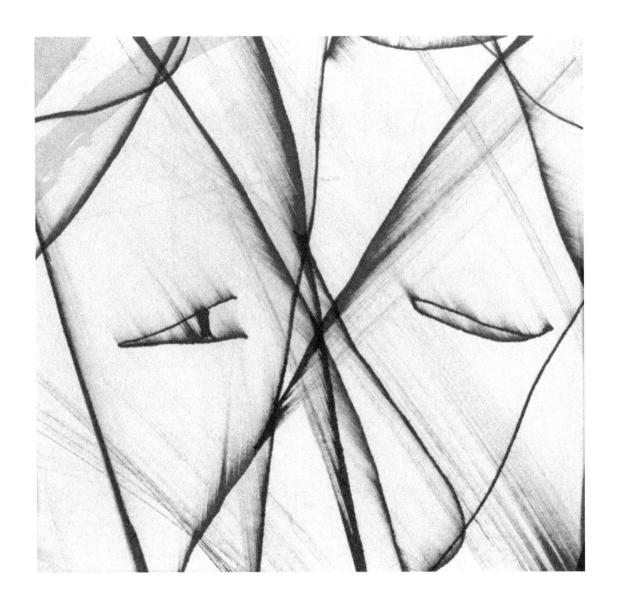

Seventy

My words are easy to understand
and easy to fulfill.
Yet, no one in the world understands them
or fulfills them.

My words have an ancestor,
and my actions are under control.
Because people hold on to their own knowledge (ignorance),
they do not know me.
Those who know me are few.
Yet, this only increases my worth.
Therefore, the wise person wears plain clothing
and carries the jade within his heart.

70

My directions are easy to comprehend
and easy to follow.
But there is no one who comprehends them
and no one who follows them.

My words go back to an ancient source.
My actions have a governor.
Since people refuse to relinquish
artificial learning,
they do not see me.
There are only a few who comprehend me.
There are many who would abuse me.
Therefore, the spiritual person
wears the ordinary clothing on the outside
but keeps the treasure in his heart.

Seventy-One

To know through ignorance is the finest good.
To think you know is a kind of sickness.
Only when you get sick of sickness,
can you become free of sickness.
The wise person is not sick
because he is sick of sickness.
Thus, he is not sick.

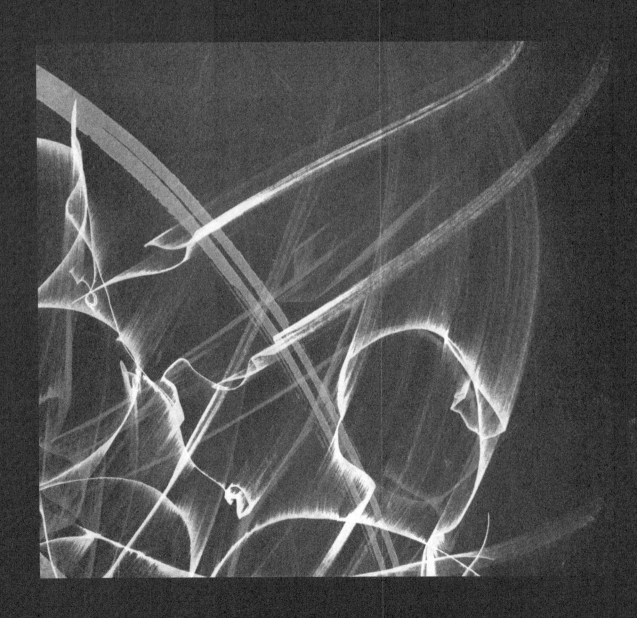

71

To have experience
of what cannot be taught is priceless.
Not having this experience is being left with
a gnawing, unanswered question that will not go away.
Only when you become weary from
the unchangeabilty of your life,
will you free yourself from this
gnawing, unanswered question.
The spiritual person
no longer has an unanswered question
because he knows the direction of his life.
Therefore, he does not suffer from having
an unanswered question.

Seventy-Two

When people have no fear of authority,
then a great fear descends.

Do not make narrow dwelling places for them
or trouble their lives.
If you leave them be, they will not tire of you.
Thus, the wise person has learned about himself
but doesn't seek renown.
He loves himself but does not consider himself
of much importance.
He chooses the one and discards the other.

72

When there is no respect for the lawful powers,
surely there will be some disastrous event.

Do not constrict peoples lives
with tiny and unpleasant spaces to live in.
Stop harassing them all the time,
and they will not become fed up with you.

Even though the spiritual person knows himself,
he doesn't make a display of it.
Though he takes good care of himself,
he is not puffed up with self-pride.
He throws away the one and takes the other.

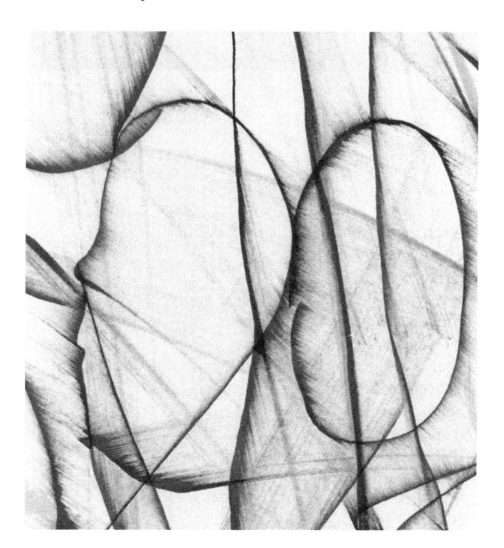

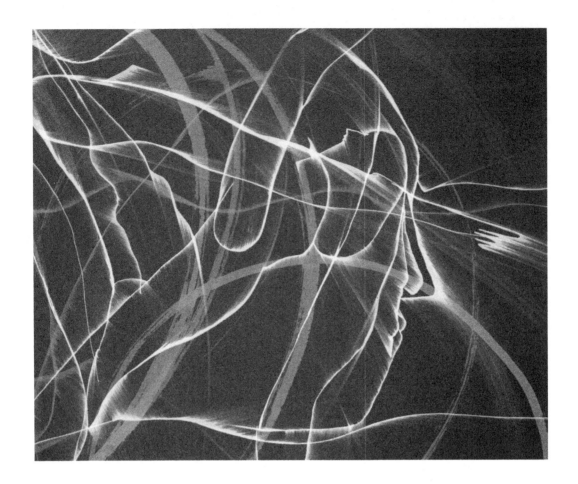

Seventy-Three

A fearless person willing to risk life
either kills or is killed.
A fearless person not willing to risk life
guards and protects life.
Of the two roads,
one leads to goodness, the other to injury.
Heaven will hate what it will hate
and who knows why?
Even a wise person has some difficulty with this.
Heaven's way is not to be contentious.
Yet, it overcomes.
It does not speak and yet, it answers.
It does not beckon and yet, others come to it
of their own choosing.
It seems spontaneous and yet, it follows a plan.
Heaven casts its massive net
and, even though the mesh is rough,
nothing ever slips through.

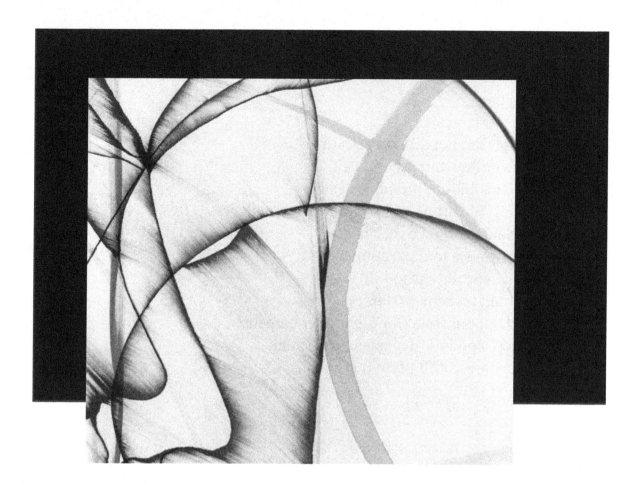

73

The reckless quickly move on;
the careful and prudent survive.
From these two paths,
one carries on
while the other becomes impaired.
The spirit dislikes what it will.
For what reason? No one really knows why.
Even a spiritual person must be careful.

The way of the spirit is not quarrelsome.
Yet, it subdues everything.
It doesn't use words; yet it communicates.
It doesn't tantalize; yet it attracts.
It appears disorganized; yet it has a method.
The spirit sends out its messages,
and everyone listens to some degree.

Seventy-Four

If the people are not afraid of death,
why make hollow threats of death.
And if the people are afraid of death,
and if you could arrest and kill all the wrongdoers,
who would dare to take the chance?
There is always a lord executioner
whose responsibility is to kill.
If you should take the executioner's place,
it's like chopping wood for the master carpenter.
If you chop wood for the master carpenter,
the chances are you'll hurt your own hands.

74

There always are a few people
who will go beyond rules, regulations
and threats of punishment.
Why attempt to frighten them with death?
There always are a majority of people
who will follow the rules and regulations.
Why burden them with harsh laws?

If you spend your life judging and condemning others,
it's like cutting parts off your own hand.

Seventy-Five

The people go hungry
when their rulers eat up everything in taxes.
That is why they go hungry.
That is why they are so hard to handle.
When rulers intervene, the people become hard to handle.
If the people are not afraid of death,
it is because their rulers are greedy
and want everything for themselves.
That is why they treat death lightly.
It is wiser not to expect too much from life
than to treasure life too highly.

75

Increase the taxes.
Help the rich to become richer
and watch the masses starve.
Why are the masses so resistant?
Is it not from all the tampering which goes on.
If they are not fearful of death,
is it not from greedy politicians
and self interest groups
who want the power and wealth for themselves.
Is it not because people's dreams about life are shattered
that they lose all hope in life.

It is better to take your dreams lightly
rather than to cherish them too much
and bring anguish to yourself.

Seventy-Six

A man is born gentle and weak
but dies rigid and stiff.
A plant enters life soft and tender
but dies brittle and dry.
Thus, the rigid and stiff are associates of death
while the gentle and weak are associates of life.
Therefore, the army that won't bend
won't be victorious.
A rigid tree calls out for the ax.
Thus, the stiff and unbending are below
while the gentle and weak are above.

76

We are born soft and vulnerable
but in death we are hard and unyielding.
Grass and trees are flexible and yielding in life
and fragile and dry in death.
Therefore, the hard and unyielding
are travelers in death,
and the flexible and yielding
are travelers in life.

The strong tree gets the ax.

Strong weapons are unyielding things
and really win nothing.
Thus, the hard and unyielding are beneath.
The soft and vulnerable are high up.

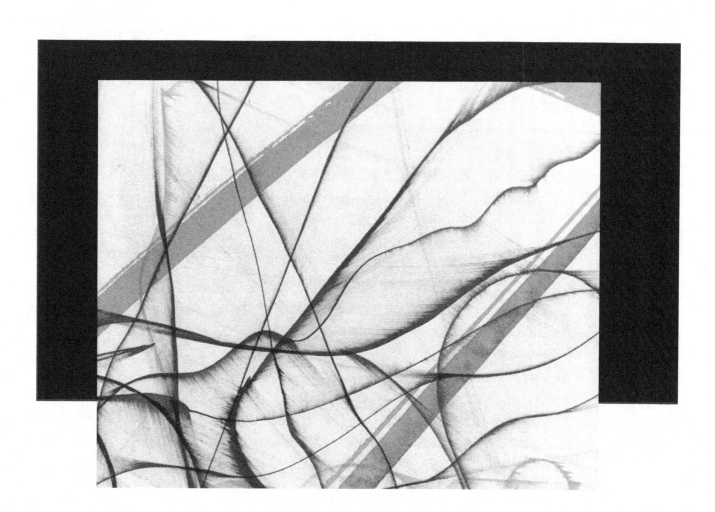

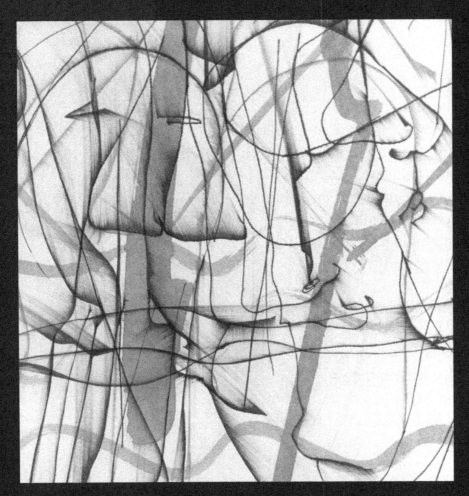

<u>Seventy-Seven</u>

Heaven's way resembles bending a bow.
From on high, it's pushed downward.
From down below, it's raised up.
It takes from those who posses too much.
It gives to those who haven't enough.
Heaven's way is to take from what has too much
and to give to what hasn't enough.
Man's way is otherwise.
He takes from those who haven't enough
and gives an offering to those who already have too much.
Is there anyone who gives his own surplus
to the kingdom?
Only the man who has the way.
Therefore, the wise person receives and gives benevolence
but doesn't ask for any thanks.
He does his job and takes no credit.
This is because he does not wish to be considered
superior to others.

77

The way of the spirit
is like the stringing of a bow.
The top is driven down; the bottom is uplifted.
From those with surplus, it obtains.
From those lacking, it bestows.

It is the way of the spirit
to obtain the surplus from what is excessive
and to give it to what is lacking.

The way of man is the contrary.
He takes from the lowly
and bestows it on the highborn.
Who is it who will bestow his dividends
on the world?
Only one who has the Tao.
Thus the spiritual person helps the world
and doesn't ask for anything in return.
He completes his work and goes on to something else.
He doesn't wish to display his value to others.

Seventy-Eight

In this world there's nothing gentler
or weaker than water.
Yet, there is nothing like it for attacking
the hard and rigid.
Nothing can alter it.
Everyone knows it is the weak that overcomes the strong,
and the soft that overcomes the hard.
Everyone in the world knows this,
but no one seems to put it into practice.
The wise person says:
he who takes upon himself the impurities of the state
is suitable for offering sacrifices to the gods
of earth and grain.
He who takes upon himself the misfortunes of the state
is suitable to rule the whole kingdom.
Straight words sometimes seem bent.

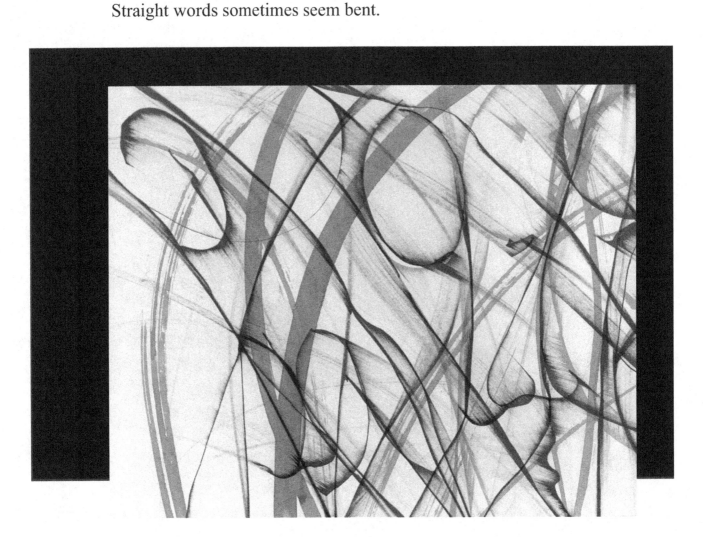

78

There isn't anything softer or more compliant than water.
There isn't anything better for winning over
the hard and unyielding.
Since it is unique, it is special.
All the world realizes that the passive
overcomes the strong,
and the compliant overcomes the unyielding.
All the world realizes but no one utilizes the knowledge.
Therefore, the spiritual person says:
the one that is willing to bear
the shame and grief of the nation is the one
who will be right for leading the nation.
Forthright words seem inconsistent.

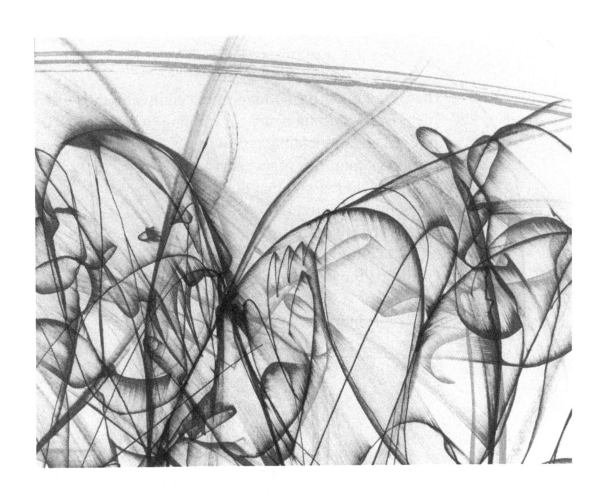

Seventy-Nine

Between two bitter enemies who make peace
some enmity is certain to remain.
How can good come of this?
Thus, the wise person
fulfills his part of the agreement
but does not demand payment from the people.
The man of goodness brings about agreement.
The man of enmity brings death.
It is heaven's way to be impartial.
It is eternally with the man of goodness.

79

When there is a reconciliation between hostile enemies,
there is going to be animosity that remains.
How can this make things better?

Although the spiritual person
holds the letter of indebtedness,
he does not ask for satisfaction.
The good man is for peace.
The hateful man is for quarreling.
It is the spirit's way not to take sides.

But it is always on the side of goodness.

<u>Eighty</u>

Let's say there is a small state with few inhabitants
where the people have access to ten
to a hundred times the resources that they will ever need.
The people will take death seriously
and not travel too far away.
And although there are boats and carriages,
no one uses them.
Although they have armor and weapons,
there is no occasion to show them.
Let the people tie knots in rope instead of writing
and enjoy their food
and make beautiful clothing
and find satisfaction in their homes.
Although neighboring states
are within sight of one another,
although you can hear the dogs barking
and the cocks crowing from both sides,
the people grow old and will die,
but they don't travel
or come into conflict with the other side.

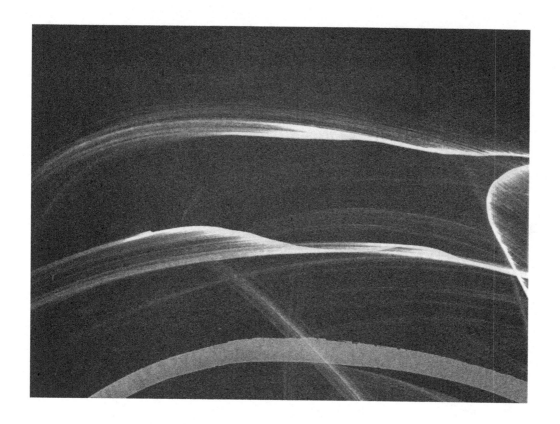

80

If the nation is small in size and number,
even though the people could increase arms and troops
ten to a hundred times over, they do not use them.
Because the people value their lives,
they do not stray far from home.
Even though there are vehicles for travel,
they are reluctant to use them.
Even though they have weaponry,
they do not display them.
Instead of writing, the people will return
to the tying of knots and the oral tradition.
They will have the satisfaction of wholesome food,
well-made clothing and pleasant dwellings.
Even though two nations are within sight
of each other, and you can hear the sounds
of children and animals from both sides,
during their lives
the people don't cross over to the other side.

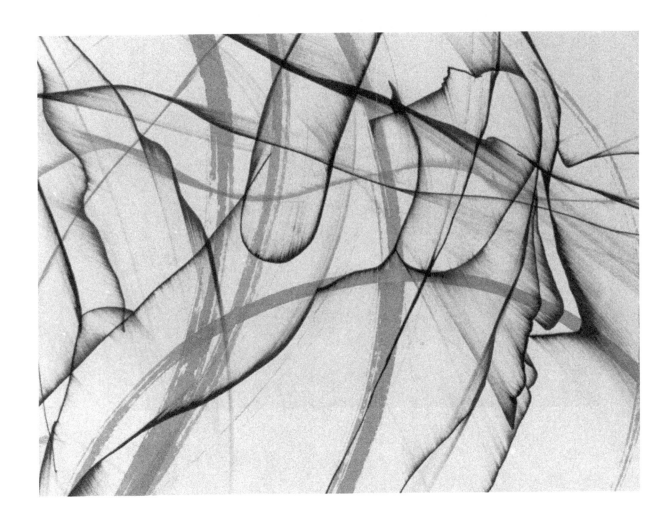

Eighty-One

True words are not beautiful.
Beautiful words are not truthful.
The person of goodness does not argue.
He who argues lacks goodness.
The wise person is not learned.
The scholar is not wise.

The wise person does not amass things for himself.
The more he gives away, the more he possesses.
The more he does for others, the wealthier he is.
Heaven's way is helpful and does not harm.
The wise person's way achieves without striving.

81

Honest words need no embellishments.
Flowery words are not honest.
A virtuous person doesn't quarrel.
A contentious person isn't virtuous.
The spiritual person is not a scholar.
The intellectual is not sound.

The spiritual person isn't greedy.
He gives away everything he has
and always has more.
Although he has given away everything,
he is truly wealthy.
The way of the spirit supports and sustains.
The Tao of the spiritual person
is the way of abundance without struggle.